What do you do
when you don't
EEL LIKE
doing what you're doing.

Cover art work by Nick LeGuern.

All Scripture quotations are from the King James Version of the Holy Bible. Capitalized and italicized words are for author's emphasis only.

What Do You Do When You Don't Feel Like Doing What You're Doing? by Joy Haney
Published by Radiant Life Publications
©1994

Printed in the United States of America.

ISBN 1-880969-13-0

CONTENTS

PREFACE

On December 4, 1965, *Gemini 7* was launched with astronauts Frank Borman and Jim Lovell aboard. During their journey they set a new space endurance record, surpassing the 200-hour mark in the midst of their 14-day mission.

Ironically, on December 15, *Gemini 6* was launched. *Gemini 6* followed *Gemini 7* because on its previous launch attempt, space officials could not get the rocket off the ground.

A small plug—worth less than a dollar—forced the delay, costing an estimated $100,000. Space agency officials said they were unsure as to how the plug fell out. When the metallic plug, which was supposed to be pulled free by a lanyard when the rocket lifted about six inches off the pad, plunked out early, it caused an electrical relay to close. This prematurely started the mission programmer, and since no lift was evident, a block house sequencer system automatically turned off the rocket motors.

One tiny plug stopped a rocket from soaring into the sky.

As one plug caused so many problems and expenses, the same thing can happen to the human body. One spirit of discouragement or weariness can cause you not to be able to lift off the launching pad. It causes your feet to drag on the ground instead of soaring, but it can be fixed!

You as a reader will probably recognize yourself in certain parts of this book, if not in all of it. **Weariness is caused by many things**. This book will explore and probe into those things. It will give hope, both factual and spiritual advice, and carry the reader to a new understanding of this modern-day problem that plagues so many, but for which there are workable answers.

Anyone who ever accomplished any great thing experienced times of frustration and weariness before he finally made it. This book is written to those who intend to achieve and win—no matter what! It will help you keep on keeping on even when you would rather do otherwise.

Mediocrity is a plague that inflicts itself on those who will let it, but excellence is a way that beckons all to higher things, causing one to dream a dream even when surroundings are desolate. The challenge is before you—do not give up, but keep reaching for excellence and achievement in God, for He is with you!

What do you do when you don't *f*EEL LIKE doing what you're doing.

J O Y   H A N E Y

"He giveth power to the faint; and to them that have no might he increaseth strength" (Isaiah 40:31).

"'For Christ's sake' should be whispered in our heart at the hardest of our duties and along the darkest of our way."

Raleigh

1

Weary?

"And Rebekah said, I am weary" (Genesis 27:46)

When the Duke of Wellington led the English forces against those of Napoleon at the Battle of Waterloo, news of the history-making battle came by sailing vessel to the south coast of England, and a signal was sent by semaphore overland toward London. On top of the Winchester Cathedral, the semaphore began to spell out the eagerly awaited message. A dense fog began to settle down just as the words "Wellington defeated" were finished. The semaphore could no longer be seen, and the heartbreaking news of Wellington's defeat spread throughout London.

After the fog lifted though, the semaphore became visible again. This time it spelled out the complete message of the battle: "Wellington defeated the enemy!" Sometimes when in a battle, your brain receives only part of the signal: defeat, weariness, frustration and loss. You fight so long and hard, but seemingly you are not getting anywhere. You sink in despair and wonder if you will ever win. This is when you become weary. The enthusiasm is gone, the marching bands have gone home, the crowd has dispersed, the last note has sounded, and the noise of the crowd has become still and quiet. "What is the use?" you cry deep within. "I've tried so hard, and now this. I'm weary of everything: the pressures, the daily grind, problems of the people that I rub shoulders with, and feeling tired all the time. If I could just get away and rest somewhere."

The first part of the above story is what this book deals with: when things look grim and circumstances cause you to feel defeated and weary. What do you do when you do not FEEL like doing what you are doing? When no one is patting you on the back, relationships have gone sour, there seems to be a devil on every corner, and everything that could go wrong seems to be going wrong; you are just tired, tired, tired. Exhausted describes you well!

There is just something about the weariness of exhaustion, when you try so hard and nothing seems to be working, that knocks you in the stomach and takes your breath away. You just try and try, working and pushing and toiling all through the night, and still nothing happens. What do you do?

There were five of us: the doctor; the nurse; my son-in-law, John, our childbirth assistant, Rachel; and myself, standing in a delivery room in Dameron Hospital around the bedside of my fourth child, Elizabeth, who was having her first baby. The nurses and everyone involved finally realized this was not a normal delivery. She had three days of labor at home and then had been in the hospital for twelve hours, and was weary from it all.

On top of that she had several complications which made it all the more wearisome. When she finally got to the point of actual delivery she was so weak it was difficult for her to push the baby from the birth canal out into the world. Her utter weariness affected her performance.

The doctor, sensing the problem, came in and gave us hope. She organized a team effort with the five of us around the bed working together crying, "Push harder than you've ever pushed before." Elizabeth, as well as the rest of us, gained new strength. It was like we had caught our second wind. When the baby was born, it was a very emotional scene. We all cried, "It's a miracle!" with tears running down our cheeks.

Where had Elizabeth received her strength? Where had our weariness gone? We had checked in at 11:30 the night before, and at 12:23 p.m. the next day the baby was born. We had not had any sleep for over thirty hours and felt like falling asleep while standing on our feet. We had been exhausted and now we felt elated.

You always have more strength than you think you have. Let me be as the doctor who entered that hospital room and gave us all a little boost. Some people had been praying for the situation and the Lord sent the right person at the right time to give us that "umph" that caused us to try again resulting in triumph over a seemingly endless, exhausting situation.

This is not the time to give up or give in. You can have more strength for the days ahead and the difficult tasks that are before you. Sometimes you just have to push a little harder and catch your second wind.

Weariness is a merciless, contagious disease. It strikes anyone and everyone! It leaves no one out. It comes uninvited into the pastor's study, the executive suite, the mother's heart, the doctor's chamber; it is no respecter of persons. The key is to strike back and win, for with Christ you can win!

Weary means "having one's strength much impaired by toil or suffering; becoming tired or fatigued, and having one's patience or tolerance exhausted." It comes from the root word *wear* which means "to use up by wearing; to consume or cause to deteriorate by use; to impair, or diminish by continual attrition or scraping, such as the rocks are worn by water; to lessen or exhaust the strength of by friction or constant use."

Attrition is a noun which means "act of rubbing together; friction; act of wearing or grinding down by friction."

The friction of daily life sometimes sets your teeth on edge. You sit at a red light while racing inside. You have so many things to do that the tension causes you to feel like crying or screaming. You do not want people to think you are crazy so you smile serenely at them, while inside, you feel frustrated and weary.

Things mount up. The monotonous grind of, yes, good things, seem to grab you by the throat and squeeze the joy of life from you. You ask yourself if this is the way life is supposed to be. Where did the wonder go? Why am I so tired? You think, "If I could just get away from it all. Maybe fly to a little island and do nothing except what I want to do for one month. Swim in the ocean, browse along the beach, read books while sitting in the sun, or shop at exotic ports." Or you may dream of getting away to a little mountain cabin high in the Sierras, sitting before a fireplace, looking out the window at the beautiful white snow on the evergreen trees, or fishing in the mountain streams, cooking the catch on an open fire in the evening. It could be a dream shopping trip in Paris, or just a few days in the country away from the masses and responsibilities. The main thing is, you feel like you need to get away!

The constant rubbing together, the continual wearing away, the "always have to be there" feeling—it is like you are caught in a vice and you are being squeezed to death. You watch a child play with happy abandon chasing leaves in the wind, and you trudge along determined to get everything done on your "to do" list, or your employer's list. You think it is endless.

You can either retreat into depression and let your enthusiasm die, or you can find the answers and solve the problem of weariness. No one or nothing can make you *keep* feeling like you feel but yourself. Other people, things, and circumstances can be a contributing factor to making you feel the way you feel, but you are the final controller of your feelings.

The exception is the people who are controlled by demon power and need to be delivered of them as the man of Gadara was set free in Luke 8. He was tormented by the evil spirits. Jesus spoke to the spirits, told them to go out of the man and the man was healed. Notice what is emphasized: "Then they went out to see what was done; and came to Jesus, and found the man, out of whom the devils were departed, sitting at the feet of Jesus, clothed, and in his RIGHT MIND" (Luke 8:35).

The right mind causes you to have a quietness in your spirit, and not to be torn up inside, frustrated, feeling like ranting and raving. It brings peace even in the storm and helps you stay on track. You as a Christian have the power to pull down imaginations or thoughts in your mind that cause you to do less than your best. As you face people and situations, you will make choices that decide what rules in your mind: chaos or purpose, bitterness or forgiveness, weariness or enthusiasm.

Everyone will face negative emotions and will have to deal with them, but you have the power to soar, to be enthused and win. Weariness will come, but if you stay weary and the problems are constantly beating you on the back with no let up, no time in-between, then you definitely have a problem. This book will help you get back on track. Instead of life riding you and dragging you along, you will rise, get on top of things and take the reins of life in your hands once more. You *can* get up out of the dirt, dust, muck and mire of constant tension, weariness, and exhaustion!

You will have rainy days, just as the poet, Longfellow, wrote about in the following poem, but not every day should be rainy. Too much rain will cause flood and disaster.

THE RAINY DAY

The day is cold and dark and dreary;
It rains, and the wind is never weary;
The vine still clings to the moldering wall,
But at every gust the dead leaves fall
And the day is dark and dreary.

My life is cold and dark and dreary;
It rains and the wind is never weary;
My thoughts still cling to the moldering past,
But the hopes of youth fall thick in the blast,
And the days are dark and dreary.

Be still, sad heart! and cease repining;
Behind the clouds is the sun still shining;
Thy fate is the common fate of all;
Into each life some rain must fall,
Some days must be dark and dreary. [1]

Yes, some days must be dark and dreary, but not every day.
You should not wear the constant garments of weariness.
There is a way to rise above the tired, exhausted weariness that
plagues this generation. Sometimes in order to get the water
out of the ground, there has to be a well dug. Everything does
not always appear magically in the hand or into existence.
Magic wands are for fairy tales. Weariness does not disappear
into the air by the waving of the wand of a fairy godmother, as
happened to Cinderella. Although the Lord Jesus does touch
men and women's lives with His glory and power, and He will
erase a weary spirit, there still is effort, diligence, and self-disci-
pline involved in adopting a lifestyle that will not encourage
weariness to hang around.

16

Sometimes weariness does not come from labor or mental exhaustion, but from anxiety-filled waiting, as the next chapter will discuss.

"He that can have patience can have what he will."

Benjamin Franklin

2

Tired of Waiting

"Blessed is he that waiteth" (Daniel 12:12)

God may have placed a dream within your heart in the distant past. You have worked toward it, planned for it, and you are still waiting for it to happen. Your expectant waiting has turned into frustration, and a, "What's the use of dreaming, nothing ever happens" attitude. The weariness of waiting has made your insides feel sour, resentful and dead.

Sometimes you feel alone, feeling like everyone else is passing you by while you just plod along. While they are rejoicing over a dream come to pass, you still have seemingly nothing. You are not alone. Many people have dreams but do not accomplish them as soon as they would like to.

The Apostle Paul had a dream, but it did not happen overnight either. He was visited one night in a vision by the Lord saying, "Be of good cheer, Paul: for as thou hast testified of me in Jerusalem, so must thou bear witness also at Rome" (Acts 23:11).

Notice after Paul heard from God, he did not sit still doing nothing. He was working, doing what he was supposed to do, when God called him to greater things. The fact is, Paul heard from the Lord, but it did not come to pass for at least two more years. When it finally did happen, he went to Rome in chains as a prisoner. He certainly did not have the glory and pomp that some expect to accompany their dreams.

The key is to not become weary while waiting for that big moment, but to do everything like it was the big moment and the big moment will eventually come. Live each day like it were the last day of your life. Each moment is an important one; do not waste it.

F.B. Meyer said,

Do not try to do a great thing; you may waste all your life waiting for the opportunity which may never come. But since little things are always claiming your attention, do them as they come, from a great motive, for the glory of God, to win His smile of approval, and do good to men. It is harder to plod in obscurity, acting thus, than to stand on the high places of the field, within the view of all, and do deeds of valor at which rival armies stand still to gaze. But no such act goes without the swift recognition and the ultimate recompense of Christ.

To fulfill faithfully the duties of your station; to use to the uttermost the gifts of your ministry; to bear the chafing of the unthankful and evil; to be content to be martyrs who bore the pillory and stake; to find the one noble trait in people who try to molest you; to put the kindest construction on unkind acts and words; to love with the love of God even the unthankful and evil; to be content to be a fountain in the midst of a wild valley of stones, nourishing a few lichens and wild flowers, or now and again a thirsty sheep; and to do this always, and not for the praise of man, but for the sake of God—this makes a great life. [1]

You may not want to wait for the fulfillment of a dream,

and because of this, the constant fretfulness for the "has nots" becomes like a stone hanging around your neck. It gets heavy, bouncing against your chest as a constant reminder that things are not the way they should be, causing you to be unhappy. Your dream becomes a wearisome thing instead of a thing of hope and inspiration.

Get up today! Look into the past at those who overcame weariness and let your dream live again. **You were born to succeed!** Enthusiasm can once again pulsate through your brain instead of the heavy weight that accompanies you into the pulpit, the marketplace, the office, or whatever place your lot in life takes you.

If you study those that the world considers achievers, you will see this mark of never giving up. Consider, for instance, the controversial Michelangelo. You do not need to agree with him on how he did it or who he did it for, but you have to agree, that even in his weariness, he chose to not give up. In 1508, a sculptor by trade, he was asked to paint the ceiling of the Sistine Chapel. History records that it took him from 1508 till 1512 to complete this monstrosity of a job. Simply for a picture on a ceiling, he gave four years of his life.

He often became weary at his task. At one time he threw paint on all his figures and started over, so exasperated was he with the results. He did not paint standing up; he painted lying down on a scaffold looking up. The difficult task was mind-boggling and time-consuming. Once he did quit, but he did not give up completely. He just kept on until he finished what some art critics feel to be one of the finest paintings in the world, and this was accomplished in an awkward position on his back.

He was willing to do this for a picture that will someday pass away.

What are you doing with the dream, talents, and opportunity that the Lord has given you? Have you succumbed to mediocrity because you just could not stand the waiting? Did you settle for less, because the best was so elusive? What is keeping you from doing what you have been asked to do? Is it people, circumstances, or the condition of your own mind?

While attending Radcliffe College, Helen Keller, the deaf and blind girl, wrote the following words in her daily journal:

> There are days when the close attention I must give to details chafes my spirit, and the thought that I must spend hours reading a few chapters, while in the world without, other girls are laughing and singing, makes me rebellious; but I soon recover my buoyancy and laugh the discontent out of my heart. For, after all, every one who wishes to gain true knowledge must climb the Hill Difficulty alone, and since there is no royal road to the summit, I must zigzag it in my own way. I slip back many times, I fall, I stand still, I run against the edge of hidden obstacles, I lose my temper and find it again and keep it better, I trudge on, I gain a little, I feel encouraged. I get more eager and climb higher and begin to see the widening horizon. Every struggle is a victory. One more effort and I reach the luminous cloud, the blue depths of the sky, the uplands of my desire. [2]

When the world thought that the British were licked in World War II, they had not contended with Sir Winston Churchill. He floored them all by his audacity in the face of utter defeat. He stepped out on the balconies of time, and thundered these words:

> We shall go to the end, we shall fight in France, we shall fight on the seas and oceans, we shall fight with growing confidence and growing strength in the air, we shall defend our island whatever the cost may be, we shall fight on the

landing grounds, we shall fight in the fields and in the streets, we shall fight in the hills; we shall never surrender, and even if, which I do not for a moment believe, this island or a large part of it were subjugated and starving, then our Empire beyond the seas, armed and guarded by the British Fleet, would carry on the struggle, until, in God's good time, the New World, with all its power and might steps forth to the rescue and the liberation of the old. [3]

With that kind of belief, who could lose? It took them through to victory!

You may feel threatened by several things, but you do not have to give in to the pressures and lose. Someone once said, "The world steps aside for the person who knows where he is going." If you want to make inroads into your weariness and frustration, bring your dream back into focus. Instead of focusing on what you are invaded with or on that which surrounds and suffocates you, look up, reach up, get up and fight!

Delays are not to frustrate you; they are to refine you. They are not to squash you; they are to ripen you, helping you to grow. So grow, mature, work, dream, sing, plan, keep on until—when the time is right, it will happen. You will not have to knock doors down; they will just open.

Do not spend all your time trying to pry the door open or knock it down; do all the things that make it open on its own accord. Reach for excellence, sharpen your skills, do everything you are doing to the best of your ability. Give, and give some more, and when you feel like you cannot give anymore, watch out, for something good will soon happen if you will not give up.

Instead of saying, "I'm so tired of being tired. I'm so tired of waiting, I'm about to give up," start saying, "I'm excited in spite of! I don't know when it's going to happen, but I know it's going to happen sooner or later, if I work hard and never give up."

You may be on the verge of giving up and giving in to weariness and pressures within, but this is no time to do so; the greatest things are just ahead. What if Thomas Edison would have given up? Because he did not, he finally gave us a light bulb that worked. But if he would have grown tired of waiting and had given up, rest assured that **somebody** would have invented the light bulb. But Edison's name is associated with it because he kept on, not giving into weariness and frustration.

What are you doing with the talent the Master intrusted into your hands? When life is all said and done, what do you want the Master to say of you? He said about Mary in Mark 14, "She hath done what she could." Will you tire of waiting and give up, or will you keep Him in focus along with the dreams He gives you and do all you can do up until the time they are fulfilled? And if they are never fully fulfilled, do not let your dreams die within, for when you do, you are dead inside.

Sing while you wait, prepare, and become. Sooner or later something good will come out of it, for what you give out will come back with interest. Learn to wait without frustration.

> The heights by great men reached and kept,
> Were not attained by sudden flight,
> But they, while their companions slept
> Were toiling upward in the night.
>
> Standing on what too long we bore
> With shoulders bent and downcast eyes
> We may discern—unseen before—
> A path to higher destinies:

Nor deem the irrevocable Past
As wholly wasted, wholly vain,
If rising on its wrecks, at last
To something nobler we attain.

Henry W. Longfellow [4]

A note of caution: Be sure what you are waiting for—or getting weary over—is God's plan for your life. Become synchronized with Him! If it is His will for you, wait as long as He plans for you to wait, but do not sit around just waiting.

There is a sad story told of a young woman named Mathilde who aspired to be welcomed in big society. However, she was the wife of an ordinary French citizen. One day Mathilde's husband obtained an invitation to attend an elegant ball. The young woman borrowed from a wealthy friend a suitable necklace to wear at the state occasion. The lovely adornment received many compliments from the aristocracy of the evening, but afterwards she lost it and could not find it.

After frantically searching for the necklace and not being able to find it, her husband borrowed 36,000 francs and bought a necklace that looked exactly like the one Mathilde had worn. Mathilde returned this to her friend, telling her nothing of what had happened.

For ten agonizing years, the couple slaved to pay back the money they had borrowed. They sold their home, dismissed their servants, and lived in a slum in order to pay the debt. After it was finally paid, Mathilde saw her well-to-do acquaintance one day and confessed all, revealing the misery she had suffered in paying for the replacement. It was then that her friend explained that the borrowed necklace was only made of paste and was worth less than 500 francs.

Be sure what **you** are slaving for and becoming weary over is worth the value of your commitment. If it glorifies Christ and enriches another soul, it is! Remember, sometimes delays are good for you and obstacles can become your friend as the following poem depicts so well:

Friendly Obstacles

For every hill I've had to climb,
For every stone that bruised my feet,
For all the blood and sweat and grime,
For blinding storms and burning heat,
My heart sings but a grateful song--
These were the things that made me strong!

For all the heartaches and the tears,
For all the anguish and the pain,
For gloomy days and fruitless years,
And for the hopes that lived in vain,
I do give thanks, for now I know
These things helped me grow!

'Tis not the softer things of life
Which stimulate men's will to strive;
But bleak adversity and strife
Do most to keep man's will alive,
O'er rose-strewn paths weaklings creep,
But brave hearts dare to climb the steep.

"No road is too long to the man who advances deliberately and without undue haste, and no honors are too distant for the man who prepares himself for them with patience."

Bruyere

3

Is "Be Not Weary" a Fairy Tale?

"Be not weary in well doing" (II Thessalonians 3:13)

Did Paul really mean this? Yes! Was he a fake, a deceiver? No, a thousand times, No! He said it like this: "And let us not be weary in well doing; for in due season we shall reap, if we faint not" (Galatians 6:9).

It is apparent that if Paul talked about weariness, then someone must have been weary. Notice Paul included himself in the statement, "Let us." **Being not weary is not a fairy tale existence.** It is a state where Christ desires His children to live. The weariness that plagues so many can be changed. It is not an incurable disease. It is only temporary, if allowed to be.

It is nothing to be ashamed of, but it is something to be gotten out of as quickly as possible. The Apostle, in sharing the highlights of his life, told of all the negative things that had been a part of him. He told about the beatings, imprisonment, stonings, shipwreck, perils, and then he said, "In weariness and painfulness" (II Corinthians 11:27).

Weariness will come to all, but what is done with the weariness will determine what the outcome of a life will be. You can sit down and die inside, or you can fight back, obeying the scripture that says, "Be not weary."

How did Paul obey this? He kept his goal ever before him. He did not lose sight of eternity in the moment of trial. He kept pressing toward the mark. He was filled with truth that burned deep within him. Truth could not be quenched by the momentary; the flame was eternal within him.

George H. Hepworth said it this way: "Amid the drudgery and hardship of life keep that truth in mind and it will clear the fogs away and leave you in sunshine. We are on the road home, and the way is sometimes dark and dreary, but when we get there we shall see that every experience of earth was intended to fit us for the higher joys of heaven." [1]

A person should not feel consistently weary; this is an unhealthy condition. There should be some sunshine, excitement, and high points, but if you are in the valley of weariness, you will come out of it. The following poem eloquently describes the heart of the weary, but also gives the hope that causes the weary to press on even when he feels like giving up.

THE TOILS OF THE ROAD

My life is a wearisome journey
I'm sick with the dust and the heat.
The rays of the sun beat upon me,
The briers are wounding my feet;
But the city to which I am going,
Will more than my trials repay;
For the toils of the road will seem nothing
When I get to the end of the way.

There are so many hills to climb upward,
That I often am longing for rest;
But He who has marked out my pathway

Knows just what is needful and best.
I know in His Word He's promised
My strength will be as my day
And the toils of the road will seem nothing
When I get to the end of the way.

Cooling fountains are there for the weary;
There are cordials for those who are faint;
There are robes that are whiter and purer
Than any that fancy can paint.
Then I'll cheerfully press hopeful onward
Knowing now through each wearisome day
That the toils of the road will seem nothing
When we get to the end of the way.

Author unknown [2]

This beautiful poem indicates what is to come, but this book will help you before you get to the end of the way. There is hope for the NOW! The key is to include God. One unknown author wrote the following poem that says it well:

I cannot do it alone,
The waves run fast and high,
And the fogs close chill around,
And the light goes out in the sky;
But I know that we two
Shall win in the end—
God and I. [3]

With God all things are possible. If you only had blue skies and sunny days, you would not accomplish nearly as much as you would accomplish accompanied by pain, struggle and hardship. James C. Kinard said,

A man, watching a plumber cut up a huge chunk of lead by driving a chisel into it, remarked that it seemed easy. The workman replied that it was but that it spoiled the chisel. The spectator could not understand how soft lead could do that. The explanation was, "It takes the temper out of the steel so that it is good for nothing else. To cut much lead will ruin the finest chisel."

Soft jobs to fill, easy tasks to perform, flower-strewn pathways to travel, all take the temper out of character and make life well-nigh meaningless. There are gifted souls who know how to dig from the dust of difficulties, loneliness, or sorrow, sparkling diamonds of joy to brighten the lives of others.

In his old age, Sir Walter Scott penned some of his most famous classics to pay off a half-million dollar debt for which he was not legally responsible. Almost totally deaf and his heart burdened with deep sorrow, Beethoven composed soul-stirring symphonies. Hiding in the castle of Wartburg from enemies seeking his life, Martin Luther translated the Bible into language that the humblest peasant could understand. Blind Fanny Crosby left many hymns of comfort and inspiration. [4]

Life is not always easy. It is an uphill climb. Ascending upward always takes more strength, usually meaning struggle, and struggle begets tiredness. The difference is where the tiredness is located. It is much easier to deal with the weariness of the body than with the weariness of the mind, but they both can be helped and oft times are intertwined.

"Be not weary" is not a fairy tale! **It is a command for excellence.** Do not join the multitudes that give up when the feeling of excitement is momentarily gone, but work on getting that excitement back. It is the will of God to live with enthusiasm and not give in to weariness!

"This is no time for ease and comfort. It is the time to dare and endure."

Winston Churchill

4
Do or Die!

"Let us go up at once, and possess it; for we are well able to overcome it" (Numbers 13:30)

It is time for you just to do it! It does not matter what circumstances say to do, or if your body and mind say to give up; the key is, do it no matter what the cost! If the Lord says do something, just do it! As Paul did, ignore the beatings, the imprisonments, perils, and hunger as much as possible, and keep reaching toward. If you fall down, get up and go again. Keep on plodding; you will reach your goal, and weariness will be forgotten in that joyous moment.

During the Civil War, at the close of the first day of the battle of Shiloh, the Union had suffered severe losses. General Grant was met by his much discouraged chief-of-staff, McPherson, who said, "Things look bad, General. We have lost half our artillery and a third of the infantry. Our line is broken, and we are pushed back nearly to the river."

Grant made no reply, and McPherson asked impatiently what he intended to do. "Do? Why, reform the lines and attack at daybreak. Won't they be surprised?"

Surprised they were, and of course, General Grant won the battle. It is not good to sit for a long period and continue in weariness. It is essential to meet crises and distresses with promptness. An aggressive pushing onward attitude is better than running away, hiding from the enemy, or any thing that constantly pulls you down or away from victory.

The Old Testament gives an account of such an attack. Queen Esther was in a prominent position thinking all was well, when one day her dream world was shattered by some dreadful news. The Jews, of which she was one, were to be destroyed. When Esther found out she was going to die, she did not cave in and get hysterical. She immediately set to work to defuse the plan of the enemy. She planned well, called on her God and did what she did not feel like doing, saying, "If I perish, I perish."

She did not perish, but lived after the crisis with even more power than she had before. Notice a verse in the last chapter of the book that contains her story: "Then Esther the queen, the daughter of Abihail, and Mordecai the Jew, wrote with all authority, to confirm this second letter of Purim" (Esther 9:29).

Theodore Roosevelt said, "To do right at all times, in all places, and under all conditions, may take courage, but it pays, for the world is always looking for moral heroes to fill its high places."

The following poem describes a man of courage who is able to face defeat without retreat. It is no time to draw a sack over your head and hide, but it is time to do or die!

COURAGE

I love the man who dares to face defeat
And risks a conflict with heroic heart;
I love the man who bravely does his part
Where Right and Wrong in bloody battle meet.

When bugles blown by cowards sound retreat,

I love the man who grasps his sword again
And sets himself to lead his fellow-men
Far forward through the battle's din and heat.

For he who joins the issue of life's field
Must fully know the hazard of the fray,
And dare to venture ere he hopes to win;
Must choose the risk and then refuse to yield
Until the sunset lights shall close the day
And God's great city lets the victor in.

Ozoro S. Davis [1]

Charles Kingsley said it well: "The men whom I have seen succeed best in life have always been cheerful and hopeful men, who went about their business with a smile on their faces, and took the changes and chances of this mortal life like men, facing rough and smooth alike as it came." [2]

This well describes Daniel. On the day of his greatest trial, when he was pronounced to die, he still went ahead with his time of thanksgiving and prayer. Nothing stopped him from doing that which was right. It was just do or die.

Life is not easy, but it can sometimes be made harder by the way we approach it. There are no easy pathways. Beecher said, "There is but one easy place in this world, and that is thy grave." Easy pathways we do not ask for, just strength to walk those that we must walk. Wendell Phillips said it this way: "Christianity is a battle, not a dream." **Tiredness and difficulties always accompany battles**, but when you set your face like a flint, no matter what, you are going to win!

When life gets rough and you cannot seem to get a grip on things, when everything goes backward and you just want to throw in the towel and quit, when you are weary and tired of fighting, sometimes you just need plain ol' grit. In pioneer days they called it "sand." If a man had courage and was able to face up successfully under heavy fire or difficulties, it was said of him, "That man has sand." The following poem, taken from the *Richmond Register* many years ago, paints a graphic picture of a locomotive going uphill, and then applies it to those that would successfully make it in life.

I observed a locomotive in the railroad yards one day,
It was waiting in the roundhouse where the locomotives stay;
It was panting for the journey, it was coaled and fully manned,
And it had a box the fireman was filling full of sand.

It appears that locomotives cannot always get a grip
On their slender iron pavement, 'cause the wheels are apt to slip;
And when they reach a slippery spot their tactics they command,
And to get a grip upon the rail, they sprinkle it with sand.

It's about the way with travel along life's slippery track.
If your load is rather heavy you're always slipping back;
So, if a common locomotive you completely understand,
You'll provide yourself in starting with a good supply of sand.

If your track is steep and hilly and you have a heavy grade,
If those who've gone before you have the rails quite slippery made,
If you ever reach the summit of the upper tableland,
You'll find you'll have to do it with a liberal use of sand.

Joy Haney / What Do You Do...?

If you strike some frigid weather and discover to your cost,
That you're liable to slip up on a heavy coat of frost,
Then some prompt decided action will be called into demand,
And you'll slip 'way to the bottom if you haven't any sand.

You can get to any station that is on life's schedule seen
If there's fire beneath the boiler of ambition's strong machine.
And you'll reach a place called Flushtown at a rate of speed that's grand,
If for all the slippery places you've a good supply of sand.

Author unknown [3]

Have the toughness to fight on, even when you feel like giving up. Your days will not be without battle, weariness, and a temptation to just let go of things, but if you will hold on, you will win!

You are not alone in your state of mind. There are millions that have experienced what you are feeling. Everyone that ever did anything had their trying moments. Despair and weariness almost forced them to quit, but they just never gave up. The tendency is to feel sorry for yourself, and feel like your efforts are not appreciated anyway, so you ask the question, "Why keep on?"

When you get in such a state of mind, remember the following poem.

WHAT OF THAT?

Tired! Well, what is that?
Didst fancy life was spent on beds of ease,

Fluttering the rose leaves scattered by the breeze?
Come, rouse thee! work while it is called today!
Coward arise! go forth upon thy way!

Dark! Well, and what of that?
Didst fondly dream the sun would never set?
Dost fear to lose thy way? Take courage yet!
Learn thou to walk by faith and not by sight;
Thy steps will guided be, and guided right.

Hard! Well, and what of that?
Didst fancy life one Summer holiday,
With lessons none to learn, and naught but play?
Go, get thee to thy task! Conquer or die!
It must be learned; learn it then patiently.

No help! Nay, it's not so;
Though human help be far, thy God is nigh,
Who feeds the ravens, hears His children's cry.
He's near thee wheresoever thy footsteps roam,
And He will guide thee, light thee, help thee home.

Anonymous [4]

If you did only what you felt like doing, you probably would not get very much done. It is great to work by inspiration and excitement, but there are days when you do what you need to do simply because it is required of you. Those are the days to do it with dignity and grace, always looking ahead to the goal.

As the great Master faced that which He did not want to do, let us face said times as such. It was in the garden that He prayed a prayer of *agony AND submission*. "Father, all things are possible unto thee; take away this cup from me: nevertheless

Joy Haney / What Do You Do...?

not what I will, but what thou wilt" (Mark 14:36).

Sometimes life's destinies must be faced with resolute submission, doing what one must do, simply because there is no other choice if the best is to be the outcome. Of course, one could settle for less, and cop out on the plan, which some people do by committing suicide mentally or physically.

People who give in to a situation, and do not **discipline** their weaker instincts, will be a wreck on the road of life or a shell of what they could be. Discipline is a dreaded word to some, but yet it is a friend to those who embrace it. Discipline is training the will to do what is right. It is a training that corrects, molds, strengthens or perfects. It can be a set of rules in a department store, a code of ethics for a college, a personal value system for the individual; it can be anything which brings someone to the higher level of self-control, or obedience to better things.

For example, in a large department store, a bulletin listed the following dress code for all the employees:

SUBJECT: CURRENT DRESS CODES

Since fashion is constantly changing and there is more and more variety in clothes for both men and women, hard and fast rules or codes for dress are difficult to develop, and sometimes the "right" clothes can be a matter of an individual's taste.

The best way to describe our "code" is that extremes in anything are generally out, as well as any clothes, hair, shoes, or accessories that would make our store look like a scene from the beach, a resort, a ballroom, or a dude ranch. Those things would include hot pants, culottes, jeans, slacks and sweaters, gauchos and knickers, floor-length skirts, jump-suits, bare midriffs, string-straps for women, and jeans, turtlenecks, and other sport apparel for men. Anything else extreme, like extremely long hair or unkempt beards for men, or hats for women detract from a store's professional appearance.

Someone once said, "It's easier to get where you'd like to be if you dress like you're already there." People tend to present a total image, not only by how they act and what they do, but how they look. Dressing with dignity as well as style and flair may hasten your trip to success.

Signed, The Store Manager [5]

Every successful business requires a leader to give direction to those involved in it. The directions and instructions are not always liked, but if one is to remain in the business and become successful, then there must be self-discipline. It is no secret that discipline over self is required for one to be successful. You cannot do only what you feel like doing. If you do not feel like doing something that is the right thing to do, just do it anyway.

What if each member of the physical body rebelled against performing its own personal duties? An adult body of average weight accomplishes many things in 24 hours:

Your heart beats 102,689 times.
Your blood travels 168,000,000 miles.
You breathe 23,040 times.
You inhale 438 cubic feet of air.
You eat 3 1/4 pounds of food.
You drink 2.9 quarts of liquids.
You lose 7/8 pound of waste.

You speak 4,800 words.
You move 750 muscles.
Your nails grow .000046 inch.
Your hair grows .01714 inch.
You exercise 7,000,000 brain cells. [6]

If one of these stopped doing what it was doing, simply because it did not feel like doing it, your body would be thrown out of kilter. As the body continually does what it was created to do, as the ocean consistently sends waves in and out, as the sun shines, and as the moon gives light to the night, so must mankind continue to give his best to whatever he is called to do.

It does not matter where one is placed, to endure and not quit is the secret of survivors. In Terrence Des Pres' book, *The Survivor*, he shares the importance of doing the best one can in horrendously awful conditions. He describes the horrifying surroundings at the concentration camps under Hitler and Stalin. After learning that the motive of the camp leaders was to destroy and dehumanize their spirit, each prisoner either gave up or decided to resist and fight back. One survivor wrote,

> From the instant when I grasped the motivating principle...it was if I had been awakened from a dream...I felt under orders to live...And if I did die in Auschwitz, it would be as a human being. I would hold on to my dignity. I was not going to become the contemptible, disgusting brute my enemy wished me to be...And a terrible struggle began which went on day and night. [7]

Another survivor says,

> There and then I determined that if I did not become the target of a bullet, or if I were not hanged, I would make

every effort to endure. No longer would I succumb to apathy. My first impulse was to concentrate on making myself more presentable. Under the circumstances this may sound ludicrous; what real relation was there between my new-found spiritual resistance and the unsightly rags on my body? But in a subtle sense there was a relationship, and from that moment onwards, throughout my life in the camps, I knew this for a fact. I began to look around me and saw the beginning of the end for any woman who might have had the opportunity to wash and had not done so, or any woman who felt that the tying of a shoe-lace was wasted energy. [8]

Instead of dying, they did what they could, and somehow that magical will to live won over death.

"We acquire the strength we have overcome."

Ralph Waldo Emerson

5

Strength For the Journey

"Quit ye like men, be strong" (I Corinthians 16:13)

What is strength? It is the capacity for exertion or endurance. It is power to resist force; it is being tough. It is the power to resist attacks; it is being impregnable. Strength will give you the firmness to stand by your ideals and not let mediocrity impregnate your brain during times of crisis, weakness, or weariness.

The prophet tells us where strength comes from. "In quietness and in confidence shall be your strength" (Isaiah 30:15). When you become weary or frustrated, one of the best things to do is get away where you can be quiet. Go to the mountains, the ocean, the desert, or if that is not possible, find *somewhere* to sit still.

Robert L. Stevenson's famous quote substantiates this. "Quiet minds cannot be perplexed or frightened, but go on in fortune or misfortune at their own private pace, like a clock during a thunderstorm."

Strength is not needed for easy tasks, or days filled with fun and frivolity. Strength is needed for the times of testing and discouragement. It is not good for anyone to live without attacks or problems, for that is what strengthens the soul: the overcoming of the struggle.

Phillips Brooks, the pastor of a large congregation many years ago, once said these words:

> Do not pray for easy lives. Pray to be stronger men. Do not pray for tasks equal to your powers. Pray for powers equal to your tasks. Then the doing of your work shall be no miracle. But you shall be a miracle. Every day you shall wonder at yourself, at the richness of life which has come to you by the grace of God. [1]

Life is a gift of God. What we do with it depends on the strength with which we face life. No matter what life consists of, there is strength for the journey, for God is with us! He said, "Fear thou not; for I am with thee: be not dismayed; for I am thy God: I will strengthen thee; yea, I will help thee; yea, I will uphold thee with the right hand of my righteousness" (Isaiah 41:10).

God said He would hold up those that need strength. He knows what it means to have a rough life, full of pain and misunderstanding by those He sought to help. He did not have an easy life without any struggles. Francis Ridley Havergal said it this way:

> Never once was He gently led. He was led into the wilderness to be tempted of the Devil. He was led by men filled with wrath to the brow of the hill, that they might cast Him down headlong. He was led away to Annas; led away to Caiaphas; led into the council of the elders and chief priests and scribes; led to Pontius Pilate, and into the hall of judgment. And then, He, our Lord Jesus Christ, was led as a sheep to the slaughter; led away to be crucified! Verily, His way was rougher and darker than mine. [2]

Strength comes many times from the struggles of life. It is the storms that balance things out and make you stronger. When everything is going great for a period of time, after awhile the raging storm of weariness attacks your mind. This storm can awaken you to greater things than what you have become content with; it actually keeps you on the cutting edge. It is a cycle you go through to keep you from being destroyed by apathy.

National Geographic reported several years ago that without an occasional hurricane, the world's weather might be even worse. Fierce tropical storms play a vital part in maintaining the heat balance between the tropics and polar regions. The tropics and subtropics receive more heat from the sun than they lose by radiation. Thus, to prevent a gradual cooling of the poles and a scorching of the equatorial regions, hurricanes help keep the balance.

Mr. Gordon E. Dunn, former director of the National Hurricane Center at Miami tells us that if hurricane control were successful and none were allowed to go through their full life cycle, nature would undoubtedly find some other method of maintaining the heat balance. In his argument against hurricane control he asks the reader a startling question: "Who can say that this new method might not be even more disastrous than the hurricane?" [3]

I ask you a question: What if you were allowed to go through life never feeling pain, weariness, or encountering storms that knocked you to the ground? What kind of person would you be? You would be a disaster! It is the dark times that make the light shine even more brighter. It is the excruciating pain one suffers that makes him more sensitive to the needs of others.

The strength comes from suffering. It comes from having gone through the fire, of feeling like giving up, but not giving up. It comes from conquering. Conquering is not sitting in rocking chairs with nothing bad ever happening. *Conquering is overcoming something that tried to conquer or triumph over you.* You were made strong by the fight!

So when you pray for strength, get ready for the fight, the storms, or difficult temptations. Prepare yourself for disappointment and weariness, for surely they will come to test your mettle. Things are strengthened by testing. Untested metals are soft, as is an individual who is allowed to escape the storms and weariness of life. Ralph Waldo Emerson, the philosopher, said, "We acquire the strength we have overcome." In order to acquire, there must first be an expenditure. The more you overcome, the more you attain and the stronger you become.

President Theodore Roosevelt gave us these rich words: "I wish to preach not the doctrine of ignoble ease, but the doctrine of strenuous life." His times of struggle and weariness prepared him for the presidency. In 1884, he suffered double tragedy. On the same day his wife, Alice, died giving birth to a daughter, his mother died of typhoid fever.

At the time of these deaths, he left politics and bought two cattle ranches on the Little Missouri River in the Dakota Territory, where the hard life and endless activity of a rancher helped him recover from his sorrow. After severe snowstorms killed most of his cattle in the winter of 1885-86, he returned to New York City and ran for mayor, but was badly defeated. In 1901, he was elected President of the United States of America.

Look at your weariness and struggles with a new light. They are to prod you on to greater things, to make you balanced and strong. In your weariness, the light of your goal may flicker and become dim, but hold on to it; you will emerge stronger than ever before.

As you overcome, you will be strengthened to climb higher mountains, refined for finer purposes, and prepared for mighty challenges ahead.   Charles W. Morton, an *Atlantic Monthly* editor, once told of the Harvard freshman who came to Dean Briggs' office to explain his tardiness in handing in an assignment. "I'm sorry, sir, but I was not feeling very well," he offered.

"Young man," Briggs said, "please bear in mind that by far the greater part of the world's work is carried on by people who are not feeling very well." [4]

If you only operate according to feeling, there will be days when you will want to quit, but just keep on, for everything you do will be rewarded accordingly.

> The easy roads are crowded,
> And the level roads are jammed:
> The pleasant little rivers
> With the drifting folks are crammed.
> But off yonder where it's rocky
> Where you get a better view,
> You will find the ranks are thinning
> And the travelers are few.
>
> Where the going's smooth and pleasant
> You will always find the throng.
> For the many, more's the pity,
> Seem to like to drift along.
> But the steps that call for courage,
> And that task that's hard to do,
> In the end results in glory
> For the never-wavering few. [5]

When President Eisenhower's $81 billion budget was considered, a newspaperman wrote, "Do you have trouble visualizing a billion dollars? Think of it this way: Fewer than a billion minutes have passed since the Emperor Nero fiddled while Rome burned. To spend $81 billion would require spending at the rate of $81 a minute ever since Nero's day—in other words, throughout most of the entire Christian era." [6]

What are a few days, weeks or months of obstacles that invite you to become weary, in view of the fact that you are going to live forever, and a billion years is only the beginning? The Lord God is with you, so it is time to start acting like it. You are timeless, you will forever be with the Lord. Be not weary; just keep fighting, for the strength will come if you purpose in your heart not to give up.

"I have been driven many times to my knees by the overwhelming conviction that I had nowhere else to go. My own wisdom and that of all about me seemed insufficient for the day."

Abraham Lincoln

6

First Thing

**"I exhort therefore, that, first of all, supplications [and]
prayers be made" (I Timothy 2:1)**

Someone once said, "You must pray first and then act."
But what if you have prayed, then acted, and have also grown
weary? Jesus said, "...Men ought always to pray, and not to
faint" (Luke 18:1). So prayer should keep one from fainting or
feel like giving up, right? But what if one is praying and still
feels like giving up? Then one must go back to the thing more
important than prayer. In fact, it is the reason for prayer, and
that is *Love*.

Prayer is more than a ritual; it is communication between
God and man. In order for daily communication to be adhered
to, there must first be an attraction, or even better, there must
be love between the two parties. When the load becomes
bigger than the love, then the whole thing becomes off-balance.
First things first. Before doing, before praying, there must be
love. It has been stated that love is blind. When two are in love
they tend to float through activities, seeing only that which
strengthens their love. Duties become privileges instead of
chores when one loves someone.

Some years ago *Reader's Digest* told the story about the

little brother who needed a kidney transplant. After searching for one, the doctors found out that the older brother's kidney would work. When the two gurneys carrying the two brothers were rolled side by side into the hospital corridor on the way to the operating room, someone asked the older brother if he was afraid of the pain and complications that would result from giving his little brother one of his kidneys. The older brother looked up at his questioner and said simply these profound words, "It won't hurt, 'cause he's my brother." He was motivated by love, not duty.

There have been many great men and women that have been motivated and controlled by love rather than duty. In describing Abraham Lincoln, Mr. Wu-Tung-Fang, a former Chinese minister to the United States, said:

> To Lincoln may be applied the words which a Chinese historian uses in describing the character of Yao, the most revered and honored of the ancient rulers of China: "His benevolence was boundless, his wisdom was profound; to anyone approaching him he had the genial warmth of the sun. Though occupying the highest station, he was not haughty; through controlling the resources of the whole nation, he was not lavish; justice was the guiding principle of his actions, nobleness was written in his face." [1]

Lincoln was what he was because his heart was filled with love for his fellowmen and the desire to serve them. No matter how busy, burdened, or perplexed he was with the cares of state, he never forgot Love's way.

One of the incidents that shows his kind heart is best described in how he treated some baby birds. In a carriage with some other candidates who were out on a political campaign in the wild West, he saw in the woods near the close of the day some baby birds that had been blown out of their nest. After asking to be allowed to get down from the carriage, Mr. Lincoln picked up the tiny creatures and restored them to their little home, while the carriage passed on ahead.

Upon reaching the inn, he was asked the cause of his delay, and astonished his hearers by telling them of his humane act, declaring that, had he not returned the birdies to their mother's care, he could not sleep at night.

Someone of a haughty spirit might say, "What foolishness!" But upon closer examination of the life of Abraham Lincoln, one discovers a fine thread that weaves itself into his life day and night. It was the motivating factor called love. He loved the people.

He loved so much that the feelings of others were considered to be more important than his own. When the news of Lee's surrender reached Washington a great crowd gathered in front of the War Department office. A band played and Vice-President Andrew Johnson made a speech in which he said, "And what shall be done with the leaders of the rebel host? I know what I would do were I President. I would arrest them as traitors. I would try them as traitors, and, by the eternal, I would hang them as traitors."

Then the crowd surged over to the White House and called for the President. Lincoln appeared at an upper window and said,

> Friends, you want a speech but I cannot make one at this time. I must have time to think. If you will come here tomorrow evening I will have something to say to you. There is one thing I will do, however. You have a band with you. There is one piece of music I have always liked. For the last four years it has not been popular in the North; but now, by virtue of my prerogative as President and

Commander-in-Chief of the Army and Navy, I declare it contraband of war and our lawful prize. I ask the band to play Dixie. [2]

What a noble gesture. Where one man wanted to hang the enemy, the President was able to put all animosity behind him and play the song of the South. He was motivated by love. Many times he grew weary and tired, but he kept doing what was right because he loved so much. He loved the right, the good, and the noble.

He once said,

I know that the Lord is always on the side of the right. But it is my constant anxiety and prayer that I and this nation should be on the Lord's side.

I have been driven many times to my knees by the overwhelming conviction that I had nowhere else to go. My own wisdom, and that of all about me, seemed insufficient for the day. [3]

If the President needed prayer, what about the rest of America and the world? It is necessary for a person to pray in order for there to be a "bounce" when there are down times. You can bounce back through the power of prayer.

Theodore L. Cuyler, D.D., wisely said,

The disciples were not losing time when they sat down beside their Master, and held quiet converse with Him under the olives of Bethany or by the shores of Galilee. Those were their school hours; those were their feeding times. The healthiest Christian, the one who is best fitted for godly living and godly labors, is he who feeds most on Christ. Here lies the benefit of Bible reading, and of secret prayer.

The very act of sitting down quietly with our crucified Redeemer at His table of love has its significance. [4]

Prayer will take you through when nothing else will. It is not enough to pray, but pray for love to fill your heart. Love will keep you on course and will see things through the eyes of God. It will give you that needed shot to get you through the most difficult times. It will help you make right judgment calls. It paves the way to great things.

You will grow weary if you do not pray, but never forget, prayer begins with love. The promise found in John 15:7 speaks of unbroken fellowship: "If ye abide in me, and my words abide in you..." The intake of the Word and prayer alone builds this. If His words abide in you, then that is love with obedience: doing heroically, no matter how seemingly heavy the cross, or every known duty. If He said, "Lo, I am with you always," and "Ye shall receive power," then that is what will happen. He will be with you through the down times.

In an old book there were penned the following words with no author's name attached to them, but they are rich with wisdom:

Reproducing the life of Jesus is life's finest, sweetest, biggest business. The Master will build the atmosphere of your life. He will make your life like a garden of roses, like an island of spices. He will bring interesting experiences, great books, inspiring sermons, rich friendships, travels and sweet meditations into your life.

God's Word He illuminates for you. He will enrich your prayer life; all because He is so anxious to get into the world through your personal atmosphere. Your experience and hungerings, your purposes and ambitions, your love and sympathy, your spirit and moods, your peace and courage all have their silent power. What you are! If you are really and fully surrendered to the Master, so that He knows He can count on you, during all your life, to reproduce His precious life, be assured—He will so lead and direct you, He will so embellish your personality with the beauty and power of truth that wherever you go something will happen in other lives through what you have become in Him. Drudgery tests and trials may come in your path. These are only to add to your opportunities of growth and experience. Some of the greatest experiences of great lives have been the struggles, patient endurance and long steep climbs, where the stones were sharp and the storms severe. [5]

If prayer and fellowship with the Master brings all of those things, why so many times do we fail to pray during the times of weariness? It is essential to begin the day with Christ, no matter how you feel. The psalmist said, "Cause me to hear thy lovingkindness in the morning; for in thee do I trust; cause me to know the way wherein I should walk; for I lift up my soul unto thee" (Psalm 143:8).

Today is the best day for there to be a change. It is time now to pray, forgive, and gain back lost enthusiasm, for in praying humbly to God, a transition takes place in the mind. It is humanity plugging into divinity, resulting in an electrical current sending surges of power back to the asker.

Prayer is food to the soul. By doing it you are strengthened. By not doing it, you are weakened. Epictetus said, "In every feast remember there are two guests to be entertained— the body and the soul; and what you give the body you presently lose, but what you give the soul remains forever." [6]

Spurgeon said, "Prayer pulls the rope below and the great bell rings above in the ears of God. Some scarcely stir the bell, for they pray so languidly; others give an occasional pluck at

Joy Haney / What Do You Do...?

the rope; but he who wins with heaven is the man who grabs the rope boldly, and pulls continuously, with all his might." [7]

It is time to pull the rope and ring the bells in heaven; not only the rope, but also the kite string.

THE KITE STRING

He stood aside from his playmates,
His sightless eyes to the sky,
And the cord in his hands was tightly drawn
By the kite that flew so high.
In his big eyes, wondering, beautiful,
On his pale little slender face
There shone such a rapture, such keen delight,
That some way it seemed out of place.
And I could not forbear to pause and to ask,
"My laddie what pleases you so,
As you hold your kite in the far-off sky,
Since its motion you cannot know?"

He turned and smiled as he softly said,
And his voice with joy was full,
"I can't just explain—but it makes me glad,
When I feel that upward pull."
That Upward Pull; how it comes to us
In the daily grind of life,
How it lifts us up and gives us rest
In the weariness of strife.
When we stand bewildered, blinded, and hurt,
'Mid the fall of our cherished dream,
It is good to know that we cannot fail,
If we follow the heavenly gleam.
And never an hour may be so sad,

Nor ever a sky so dull
But we may, if we will, reach out and find
That God-given, Upward Pull.

Helen M. Wilson [8]

Why wait until you get bogged down to pray? Pray first thing. David, the singer of old, was inspired to write, "My voice shalt thou hear in the morning, O Lord; in the morning will I direct my prayer unto thee, and will look up" (Psalm 5:3). When you start your day looking up, things always go better.

If your prayers seemingly cannot get past the ceiling, then try praying with someone else. Jesus said, "Again I say unto you, That if two of you shall agree on earth as touching any thing that they shall ask, it shall be done for them of my Father which is in heaven" (Matthew 18:19). Prayer made together is very strengthening. It is well described in the following poem:

AT PRAYER MEETING

There were only two or three of us
Who came to the place of prayer—
Came in the teeth of a driving storm;
But for that we did not care.
Since after our hymns of praise had risen,
And our earnest prayers were said,
The Master himself was present there
And gave us the living bread.

We knew his look in our leader's face
So rapt and glad and free:
We felt his touch when our heads were bowed,
We heard his "Come unto me."

Nobody saw him lift the latch,
And none unbarred the door;
But "peace" was his token to every heart,
And how could we ask for more?

Each of us felt the load of sin
From the weary shoulders fall:
Each of us dropped the load of care,
And the grief that's like a pall;
And o'er our spirits a blessed calm
Swept in from the jasper sea,
And strength was ours for toil and strife
In the days that were thence to be.

It was only a handful gathered in
To the little place of prayer;
Outside were struggle and pain and sin,
But the Lord himself was there;
He came to redeem the pledge he gave—
Wherever his loved ones be
To stand himself in the midst of them
Though they count but two or three.

And forth we fared in the bitter rain
And our hearts had grown so warm,
It seemed like the pelting of summer flowers
And not the crush of storm;
"'Twas a time of the dearest privilege
Of the Lord's right hand," we said,
"As we thought how Jesus himself had come
To feed us with living bread."

Margaret Sangster [9]

To be such a marvelous thing, prayer is certainly a neglected practice. James said, "The effectual fervent prayer of a righteous man availeth much" (James 5:16). Evans Roberts said it well: "Secret intercessions make it possible for public laborers to do their work and win. They do as much for the Lord's cause who intercede like Moses on the mount, as they do who fight like Joshua in the thick of the battle. Prayer based on God's Word is the only weapon man can use to touch the invisible foe." [10] Melanchton wrote, "Trouble and perplexity drive me to prayer, and prayer drives away perplexity and trouble." [11]

"We search the world for truth, we cull
The good, the pure, the beautiful
From graven stone and written scroll,
From all old flower fields of the soul,

And weary seekers of the best,
We come back laden from our quest
To find that all the sages said
Is in the Book our mothers read."

John G. Whittier

7

Root System

"My soul melteth for heaviness: strengthen thou me according unto thy word" (Psalm 119:28)

The Chinese proverb says, "Dig the well before you are thirsty." I say, dig in the Word before the blahs and weariness become a habit. Prepare the mind before the onslaught. Aside from sin and the devil, the root of all problems is what is allowed to control the mind.

When you want to get rid of a disease, you must first get to its root cause. It is the same in dealing with the body. What controls the body? The brain. The mind controls a person's actions. So the most important thing—or the root system—is what is formed in the mind. The mind is the thing that will make the difference in your ability to overcome. In order for the mind to be strong, it must be filled with strength-giving material. It must be worked on.

If we work upon marble, it will perish; if we work upon brass, time will efface it; if we rear temples, they will crumble into dust; but if we work upon our immortal minds, if we imbue them with principles—with the just fear of God and our fellow man—we engrave on those tablets something which will brighten to all eternity (Daniel Webster). [1]

FEED THE MIND! Feed it with:

1. The Word of God
2. Communication with God
3. Great music
4. Kind acts
5. Contents of great books
6. Anything that edifies
7. Beauty

We are instructed to have the mind of Christ. "Let this mind be in you, which was also in Christ Jesus" (Philippians 2:5). In order to have the mind of Christ, there must be study and familiarizing oneself with the Word of God, for the Word will keep you when your mind is under attack from weariness.

The story is told of a drug store security guard named Louie D. Hairston of Washington, D.C. A masked bandit lunged at him with a foot-long butcher's knife. The New Testament Hairston carried in his breast pocket for spare-time reading absorbed what would have otherwise been a fatal thrust. He told the police, "He would have killed me except for the Bible."

Weariness can kill you the same as a knife, but as the Bible saved Hairston, so it will save you in the moments of weariness. It is more powerful than dynamite. "For the word of God is quick, and powerful, and sharper that any twoedged sword, piercing even to the dividing asunder of soul and spirit, and of the joints and marrow, and is a discerner of the thoughts and intents of the heart" (Hebrews 4:12).

It will help cut out the potential crippler of the spirit of weariness. As a doctor probes the diseased brain to remove the tumor, so the Word of God probes the weary brain and removes that which would destroy. It is light, power, and strength!

What you think about all day long is what you become. If one thinks on the Word of God, then he will be successful. The Book of Psalms substantiates this over and over, beginning with Psalm 1:1-3:

> Blessed is the man that walketh not in the counsel of the ungodly, nor standeth in the way of sinners, nor sitteth in the seat of the scornful, But his delight is in the law of the Lord; and in his law doth he meditate day and night. And he shall be like a tree planted by the rivers of water, that bringeth forth his fruit in his season; his leaf also shall not wither; and whatsoever he doeth shall prosper.

Is not this pretty good insurance against failure? Can you find anything else that will give you such a guarantee? Whatsoever is done is promised to prosper, but remember that prospering is not without its challenges, bad weather, and struggles. The important thing to know is that the Word of God, when meditated on, will be the thing that will take you through to victory.

When heaviness and weariness plague you, strengthen yourself by the Word. The psalmist said, "My soul melteth for heaviness: strengthen thou me according unto thy word" (Psalm 119:28). There is nothing that compares with its power. You get more from the Bible than from any other thing on earth.

Walter F. Burke, general manager of Projects Mercury and Gemini and vice-president of the McDonnell Aircraft Corporation, declared,

> I have found nothing in science or space exploration to compel me to throw away my Bible or to reject my Savior,

Jesus Christ, in whom I trust. The space age has been a factor in the deepening of my own spiritual life. I read the Bible more now. I get from the Bible what I cannot get from science—the really important things of life. [2]

Feed your mind with it. It is a gold mine of treasures. John Quincy Adams, the sixth President of the United States, said,

I have for many years made it a practice to read through the Bible once a year. My custom is to read four or five chapters every morning immediately after rising from my bed. It employs about an hour of my time, and seems to me the most suitable manner of beginning the day. In what light soever we regard the Bible, whether with reference to revelation, to history, or to morality, it is an invaluable and inexhaustible mine of knowledge and virtue. [3]

President George Washington said, "It is impossible to rightly govern the world without God and the Bible." Even so, it is impossible to govern our own life without God and the Bible. The Word is the root system, the very thing that lets the mind receive food to nourish the rest of the body, soul, and spirit.

Woodsmen report that, roughly estimated, the root spread of a tree equals the spread of its branches, through there are exceptions to this. About one-tenth of a tree is concealed in its roots. The combined length of the roots of a large oak would total several hundred miles. A birch tree, though less sturdy than many other trees, can lift a boulder weighing twenty tons. A good root system serves two purposes in the tree's development. First, it functions as an anchor. Second, the roots collect moisture, without which the tree could not thrive.

Does it matter what is fed into the root system of a tree?

Joy Haney / What Do You Do...?

The upper tree is an indication of how healthy the root system is. If there is a lack of food or water going to the roots deep within the ground, the leaves start to die, branches dry up and break off, and eventually the whole tree dies.

This is what happens if the mind is not fed properly with the Word, beauty, contents of great books, great music and other things that edify. It is impossible to remain healthy and productive without properly feeding and watering the root system, for the mind controls the emotions, heart and soul.

Just as a tree will die without food and moisture, so a mind will become dead, weary and lifeless without feeding it the Word of God.

If a person is drying up from a lack of faith because of what is fed the mind, then he will die. Worry and anxiety will become as a disease in the mind. Worry is a choker of life. It destroys the good. If you listen to everything that is said by others instead of to the Word of God then you will worry and be choked.

Have you ever looked closely at the word *weary?* What word do you see within it? *EAR.* The ear feeds the mind, as do the eyes. What are you listening to, what influences you? One can become weary because of what the ear listens to, just as he can become strong by listening to the Word of God. Guard your ears and eyes. Be careful of what you digest into your mind, for what you think about all the time is what you become. It is not wise to counsel with only your own thoughts. Hold counsel with the Word. Be careful of closing your mind to greater things just because they are unfamiliar to you.

When Thomas Edison thought he had discovered a way to record and reproduce the sound of a human voice on a machine, he called in a model maker. Handing the man a rough pencil sketch of his idea, he asked that a working model be built.

The man surveyed the sketch, then declared, "Impossible.

That thing will never work. No one has ever made a machine that could talk."

Instead of accepting this verdict, Edison determinedly said, "Build what I have sketched here and let me be the loser if it doesn't work."

The Word of God instructs us over and over to meditate on the law of the Lord. In doing so there is promised success. But many times, because of circumstances, man is tempted to say, "Impossible," just because it does not make sense that some printed words on a page could have such power. The difference is, these are not words from just any man printed on a page, but they represent the mind of God. The Word is God speaking to man, and it is proven, irrevocable, and established forever and ever.

The Word will stave off continual weariness, establishing a root system that will not fail in the most devastating storm of life. Feed the root system and the root will feed you! The greatest thing you can do for yourself and others is to become RICH! Rich not in the world's goods, but rich in the Word of God. This is the way to true riches, blessing, and favor. He that seeks the wisdom from above is promised to be divinely guided in all that he does. His steps cannot go wrong because the Word promises it to be so!

> My son, forget not my law; but let thine heart keep my commandments: For length of days, and long life, and peace, shall they add to thee. Let not mercy and truth forsake thee: bind them about thy neck; write them upon the table of thine heart: So shalt thou find favour and good understanding in the sight of God and men. Trust in the Lord with all thine heart; and lean not unto thine own understanding. In all thy ways acknowledge him, and he shall direct thy paths (Proverbs 3:1-6).

The way to acknowledge God is to listen to what He says. He says it in the Book!

In the first major address of InterVarsity Christian Fellowship's 1976 *Urbana* convention, IVCF President John W. Alexander emphasized his belief that the Bible "is the infallible revelation of the infallible God—which means that it is entirely trustworthy and reliable." He told the students, "Our attitude toward the Scripture is desperately important."

When America's colleges were first formed, the Bible was the main book on campus. John Harvard, founder of the first college, Harvard College, had three rules adopted in 1646 for each student to obey. Number three was so effective that 52% of the 17th century graduates became ministers. It read, "Everyone shall so exercise himself in reading the Scriptures twice a day that they be ready to give an account of the proficiency therein, both in theocratical observation of languages and logic and in practical and spiritual truths."

Then in 1787, Thomas Paine, an immigrant to America, wrote *The Age of Reason,* which scoffed at Christianity. He said of his masterpiece, "This will destroy the Bible. Within 100 years, Bibles will be found only in museums or in musty corners of second-hand bookstores." His book was published in 1794, but it brought him so much misery and loneliness that he once said, "I would give worlds, if I had them, had *The Age of Reason* never been written."

Though Paine tried to fight the Bible, and though others fight it unknowingly by not reading or ignoring it, the Bible still remains the most powerful Book on earth. It is the most neglected source ever given to mankind. It virtually can open up that which is closed, consistently inspire, and bring about miraculous changes. Yet many people continue to live humdrum lives full of misery and pain, all because they do not fill their mind with it, reinforcing the root system which is their controlling force.

Will you join John Harvard and pore over the Word daily, letting your root system be strengthened? Or will you throw away the power that is available to you, and unknowingly join Thomas Paine in disrespecting the Word by neglecting it? If you want power, read it! If you want misery, neglect it! It is that simple. A man or woman alone with their own thoughts and the thoughts of others lead futile, desperate lives. But those who fill their mind with wisdom from the mind of God are filled with fire, motivation and dynamite.

"Words are things, and a small drop of ink,
Falling like dew upon a thought, produces
That which makes thousands, perhaps millions think."

Lord Byron

8

Feed the Mind

"Be ye transformed by the renewing of your mind"
(Romans 12:2)

Solomon penned the wise words, "For as he thinketh in his heart, so is he" (Proverbs 23:7). Emerson, the philosopher, concurs with this. He said, "You are what you think about all day long." When your thoughts are tired, your body is tired. When your mind has grown stale, bored, and listless, the same thing happens to the body. You must constantly feed the mind, for that is your control system. You are never beaten until you are first beaten in your mind. As a college instructor, often I use the following poem given to me quite a few years ago, which says it well.

If you think you are beaten, you are.
If you think you dare not, you don't
For success begins with a person's will.
It's all in the state of the mind.

You've got to think high to rise
In order to win the prize

For sooner or later the man who can
Is the one who thinks he can.

Can't never did a thing, but *can* can. Paul said boldly under
the inspiration of the Holy Spirit, "I can do all things through
Christ, which strengtheneth me" (Philippians 4:13). Who has
control of your mind—God or failure? Your mind is where the
problem is. You are thinking the wrong things when you feel
like everyone is against you, that life is not worth living, but
instead is drab, desolate, and discouraging. You are beaten in
your mind. It is not what happens to you that matters, but how
you react to that which happens to you. Your mind controls
how you react.

Nothing can get you down but yourself. When you allow
the wrong things to rest in your mind and then you subsequently
feed on them, the result is a breakdown. Everything gets
thrown out of gear. Confusion enters and feelings become blue,
frustrated and weary. You become like a sinking ship
floundering in the ocean. *But it does not have to be that way!*

All the water in the world.
However hard it tried,
Could never, never sink a ship
Unless it got inside.

All the hardships of this world,
Might wear you pretty thin.
But they won't hurt you, one least bit
Unless you let them in.

Author unknown [1]

Keep the spirit of weariness out of your mind! It is best not to let it come into your mind, but if it does, something good can happen in spite of it. Sometimes when you get stale, or are in a rut doing a good thing, weariness can cause you to drop back a little and look at things more closely. You have the opportunity to re-examine, re-group, and gain your second wind for another thrust forward. All is not lost if it enters your mind. Good can come out of it if you allow it to. It is important to learn how to control what goes into your mind, and what is allowed to stay there, for it is your control center.

"A truly great person is one whose body has been trained to be the servant of his mind; whose passions are trained to be the servants of his will; who enjoys the beautiful, loves truth, hates wrong, loves to do good, and respects others as himself." [2]

Trained to be servant of his mind. If this is true, then it is essential to have a mind that is filled with goodness, truth, confidence and God. Think big thoughts, for you are what your thoughts are.

A caption on an advertisement several years ago in a large magazine read, "You're as big as you think!" The picture was of a boy gazing into the future. In the background there was a whirling planet and a rocket bursting out into space. The caption was explained in one short paragraph: "Only a boy. But his thoughts are far in the future. Thinking, dreaming, his mind sees more than his eyes do. So with all boys...Vision, looking beyond the common place, finds new things to do. And growth, as it always must, follows where mind marks the way."

You can lock a person in a prison, but you cannot lock up his mind. John Bunyan was locked in a Bedford jail and wrote the most popular book written in the English language, *Pilgrim's Progress.* Paul, the Apostle, locked in a prison, wrote epistles that are still being read.

It is essential to feed the mind things that will build and edify the person. As the person is inspired, then he inspires each person he comes in contact with. A life that is void of inspiration and beauty soon becomes dull, listless and a bore. If your mind is full of beauty and the love of beautiful things, it will not have as much room to harbor thoughts that are sent out to hurt and injure. The walls of your mind will be strengthened with inspiration that will enable you to fight back when weariness attacks.

Take the time to look up at the stars at night. What vastness of great thoughts may be germinated merely by thinking and speculating on the vast universe and God, the Creator. Look at the many beautiful things: colorful orchards, mountains, flowers, birds, and trees. You must take time to mentally breathe beauty into your mind, even in the midst of such a war-torn, violent generation. Let not only God's beautiful creation nurture you, but let the beauty of Jesus be part of your daily meditation. Focus on the beauty instead of the garbage.

Paul instructed Timothy to meditate, which is to think upon or feed the mind with something. "Meditate upon these things; give thyself wholly to them; that thy profiting may appear to all" (I Timothy 4:15). Notice his profiting came from what he meditated upon.

A man is as great as the dreams he dreams,
As great as the love he bears;
As great as the values he redeems,
And the happiness he shares.
A man is as great as the thoughts he thinks,
As the worth he has attained;
As the fountains at which his spirit drinks
And the insight he has gained.
A man is as great as the truth he speaks,
As great as the help he gives,

Joy Haney / What Do You Do...?

As great as the destiny he seeks,
As great as the life he lives.

C.E. Flynn [3]

Great lives are the result of great thoughts, for what one speaks, does, and accomplishes first originates as a thought. When just a little girl walking in the mountains with my mother and father, I complained to them of the sharp objects in the road that were hurting my foot. Mother wisely said, "Take your shoe off. Let us see if anything is inside first." Sure enough there was a very small rock that had imbedded itself into the lining of my shoe.

So often we view life through the pebbles that are imbedded in our mind. The mental problems become painful objects that poke and hurt us every way we turn. When we seek to get the hard pebble out of our mind, then the pain is relieved.

The most important thing you can do for yourself is to feed the mind good things and to guard it from that which is hurtful. Whatever you do with your mind is what you do to yourself and to others. As you are careful about the money you spend and the bed you sleep in, be even more careful about the mind God has given you. Nourish and cleanse it, build and inspire it, for it is given to you to bring you closer to God.

"Let this MIND be in you which was in Christ Jesus," instructs the Apostle Paul in Philippians 2:5. The mind of Christ was a humble, obedient, and submissive mind to the greater will of God. The mind is not given to self-destruct or to be used to hurt others. It is given so that the Lord God may be glorified in your living, and that others may be blessed by your contribution to life. This is why it is so important to live an abounding and abundant life, no matter what the circumstances are. You cannot do this with a mind filled with junk! So start cleaning out the pebbles and little rocks that obstruct abundant living in Christ!

"Solitude is essential to the healing of a weary spirit."

Anonymous

9

Hide

"In the time of trouble, He shall hide me" (Psalm 27:5)

If you do not take the time to hide away, you will definitely be forced to hide, either with a temporary breakdown or permanently, six feet under the ground. Is this biblical? When life got to be too much for Jesus, He hid himself. "They took up stones to cast at him; but Jesus hid himself" (John 8:59). When you feel the stones of life pelting you until you feel like you cannot go on, it is time to hide.

This was not the first time Jesus tried to hide. Another time was when He was speaking to the multitude. "These things spake Jesus, and departed, and did hide himself from them" (John 12:36). Other times He tried to hide, but could not. "And from thence he arose, and went into the borders of Tyre and Sidon, and entered into an house, and would have no man know it: but he could not be hid" (Mark 7:24). That particular time they found Him.

It is essential to get away from the press of the crowd or the press of life and hide for a short period. It renews, strengthens, and prepares one for the remainder of the journey. Short pauses do more for an individual sometimes than one long vacation. A 24-hour break will do wonders. That is if one will truly hide, relax, and change pace from the normal speed.

This advice, of course, is to those that are busily engaged in work that is constant, sure and full of pressure. This is certainly not to those who sit around twiddling their thumbs wasting time. They are hiding from work, which will breed weariness and boredom faster than anything.

There is something secretive about hiding. It closes the door on pressure, trouble, and responsibility. It makes time for listening to the sounds that are hidden during the rush of work. It is important to listen to the sounds of birds singing, the rush of a mountain stream, the roar of the ocean, the call of the seagulls, or the quiet sounds of the meadow. These are the many sounds of nature that bring balance and beauty back to our stretched minds and taunt nerves.

When you are in trouble emotionally because of weariness, that is when God promises to hide you. "For in the time of trouble he shall hide me in his pavilion: in the secret of his tabernacle shall he hide me; he shall set me up upon a rock" (Psalm 27:5).

That rock is Christ Jesus! He will hide you away in His presence and surround you with His music: the music of peace, quietness, and serenity. "In thy presence is fulness of joy; at thy right hand there are pleasures for evermore" (Psalm 16:11). That is why it is so essential to hide away in a secret place every day with Him! It is important to not only take time to hide with Him daily, but also to rest from the daily grind. You need to take a break! Sometimes small breaks are enough, and when those are not enough, then you need a longer period of time. That is when you need to get away from everything even if it is just 24 hours.

Coffee breaks are as natural as breathing to this generation, but it was not always so. There was a man who saw the weariness of the men in a steel plant, and how their footsteps lagged toward the last few hours of the day. He suggested taking twelve-minute breaks. He told them to do nothing but relax. After the trial period of this experiment it was discovered that the men accomplished more with the breaks than they did without the breaks. So coffee breaks as we know them today began.

Arthur C. Benson says it like this:

The essence of happy living is never to find life dull, never to feel the ugly weariness which comes of overstrain; to be fresh, cheerful, leisurely, sociable, unhurried, well balanced. It seems to me impossible to be these things unless we have time to consider life a little, to deliberate, to select, to abstain. [1]

You must take time to come apart from the hustle and bustle of life. It is essential to have times to look forward to where the word *hurry* has been erased. If hurry is constantly your guide, you will eventually be forced to hide. Then it may be too late to enjoy the things that were once important to you, but were gone before you learned to pace yourself and get in tune with the Creator.

Take time to smell the flowers, to walk along the ocean, to gaze at the sunsets, to sit quietly on a large stump in the cool mountain air, or yes, even take time to let friendships flourish. When a person becomes too busy that his family and friends are forgotten, then he is too busy. Take a break! Go eat homemade ice cream with a friend in the summer, or linger around a fireplace enjoying hot spiced apple cider in the winter. A person whose nose is constantly in a brief-case, or whose fingers are constantly dictating to a computer, will soon lose the glow of life.

A FRIEND—TOO LATE

Around the corner I have a friend,
In this great city that has no end,
Yet days go by and weeks rush on,
And before I know it a year is gone
And I never see my old friend's face:
For life is a swift and terrible race.
He knows I like him just as well,
As in the days when I rang his bell,
And he rang mine; we were younger then,
And now we are busy, tired men—
Tired with playing a foolish game,
Tired with trying to win a name,
"Tomorrow, say, I will call on Jim,
Just to show I am thinking of him."
But tomorrow comes and tomorrow goes,
And the distance between us grows and grows,
Around the corner yet miles away.
"A telegram, sir!" Jim died today!
And that's what we get, and deserve in the end:
Around the corner, a vanished friend.

Author unknown [2]

Yes, it is important to take time to talk to friends, go to the
ocean, read a good book on a lazy summer day, and listen to
some great symphony music, although if this is all a person
does, then he is in grave trouble. It is an established fact that a
person that wants to hide all the time has a deep problem.
Hiding as Jesus hid should be preserved for those times of in-
between. It should act only as an interval, not a continuous act.
It is a time of renewal—letting the soul catch up with the fast

Joy Haney / What Do You Do...?

pace of the body. It is a time to hang loose, to relax, think lazy thoughts, to sleep, play, or walk along the beach—to just get away from the rigid schedules, the pull of the clock, and the multitudes that need you.

Although the need for a short time of hiding away from the press is stressed here, it does not take away from the joy of work. Work that is done with a right attitude will be enjoyed by the worker and even those around him, as well as accomplishing much more than work done grudgingly. A person who consistently faces his or her work with a gritting of the teeth and a forced will should examine the situation seriously. This is not healthy and it is not the way God intended for it to be. There definitely needs to be some changes.

Too much relaxation or hiding is not good for you. It breeds boredom and restlessness. A busy or full mind is one that stays out of trouble. George Matthew Adams said it this way:

Most of the unhappiness in this world is caused by having nothing to do. I have known people who lived under circumstances sufficient to madden many, but who, because of a cheerful frame of mind and a fine philosophy of life, were really happy. And this came about largely because of a full mind. People with much to do are rarely in trouble. It's the vacant, tumble-down minds that cause unhappiness to themselves and to others. [3]

David Grayson wrote,

Happiness, I have discovered, is nearly always a rebound from hard work. It is one of the follies of men to imagine that they can enjoy mere thought, or emotion, or sentiment. For happiness must be tricked! She loves to see men at work. She loves sweat, weariness, self-sacrifice. She will be found not in palaces but lurking in cornfields and factories and hovering over littered desks; she crowns the unconscious head of the busy child. If you look up suddenly from hard work you will see her, but if you look too long she fades sorrowfully away. [4]

A poem taken from *The Silent Partner*, expresses it well:

If you are poor—work.
If you are rich, continue to work.
If you are burdened with seemingly unfair responsibilities, work.
If you are happy, keep right on working. Idleness gives room for doubts and fears.
If disappointments come—work.
If sorrow threatens you and loved ones seem not true—work.
When faith falters and reason fails—just work.
When dreams are shattered and hope seems dead—work.
Work as if your life were in peril. It really is.
Whatever happens or matters—work.
Work faithfully—work with faith.
Work is the greatest material remedy available.
Work will cure both mental and physical afflictions. [5]

John Ruskin said, "If you want knowledge you must toil for it; and if pleasure you must toil for it. Toil is the law. Pleasure comes through toil, and not by self-indulgence and indolence. When one gets to love work, his life is a happy one."

Sometimes good hard physical labor is therapy for a tired, weary mind that is a result of working with people and their problems, sitting in an office working with computers and fig-

Joy Haney / What Do You Do...?

ures, or doing the same thing over and over that requires much mental concentration. A change of labor is good for the mind. Just getting away and doing something different from the routine of things, the grind of the expected, and attending to the needs that constantly beckon is essential.

So work hard, enjoy your work; and if you do not enjoy doing what you are doing at least half of the time, then find out why and do something about it. Then take periodic breaks from the demands of an impatient schedule and the press of the crowd.

It was said of Leonardo Da Vinci that for any sort of mechanical work he would lay aside his brush. Apart from being one of the world's greatest painters, he was probably one of the greatest engineers of his time, possessing more vision than any man who lived in his century. He probably never could have painted *The Last Supper, Mona Lisa* and his other masterpieces if he had not been willing to drop his brushes and do other work. He concentrated upon these, worked at them until he was tired, and then did something else he enjoyed for a change of pace.

So if you find yourself continually having the feeling of not wanting to do what you are doing—where once you did—then it is time to take a break and use it to feed and restore the mind. Do not forget that much of fulfillment is related to having something to do. A stream that stops flowing stagnates. A tree that stops growing dies. A human being that stops working on something that is a challenge to him dries up and becomes weary. A prolonged idle position of retreat is a threat. It is necessary to flow forward with purpose, enthusiasm, and zeal in order to combat the tired-of-being-tired syndrome.

In your times of hiding, take time to nurture yourself. Someone once said it is a good thing to give ten percent to yourself, and then you will have ninety percent for God and others. It is apparent that when you are out of kilter with self, you are out of kilter with everything else. When you feel good about yourself, are organized, rested, and on top of things, you naturally perform better in all your areas of responsibility.

No one can give you these private times but yourself. Take them, cling to them, and make your own time as sacred as time spent with others. When you keep your spirit healthy, you will feel more like helping others. So in being good to yourself, you are being good to others. When we become lean in spirit and are stretched too far, what was once a joy becomes a drudgery. That is why you need to leave some open spaces on your datebook, so your spirit can be filled. There is a richness of simplicity and wonder when one is alone away from the maddening crowd.

To keep you in good shape in between the times you have alone for yourself, develop the discipline of reading good literature daily. You must feed your mind with the best you can read because you are influenced by what you select. By stimulating yourself, you will be able to stimulate others around you.

"Put off thy cares with thy clothes, so shall thy rest strengthen thy labor, and so thy labor sweeten thy rest."

Francis Quarles

10

Rest in the Lord

**"Rest in the Lord, and wait patiently for him:
fret not thyself" (Psalm 37:7)**

What does it mean to *fret?* It means "to eat away; gnaw, to
wear away; rub; chafe, to worry; to be vexed or irritated or
have an agitated mind." Fretting causes negative stress which
causes weariness.

Why do Christians worry and fret when Paul said, "Be
careful for nothing, but in every thing by prayer and
supplication with thanksgiving let your requests be made known
unto God, and the peace of God, which passeth all
understanding, shall keep your hearts and minds through Christ
Jesus" (Philippians 4:6-7).

It is possible to work hard and yet feel rested in your mind.
Weariness can be caused by fretting instead of resting in the
Lord. You will have needs, but instead of worrying about
them, take them to the Lord with a spirit of thanksgiving
instead of a whining spirit. Believe that He *will* help you. Then
experience the peace that comes from trusting and relaxing in
God.

It all goes back to what is allowed to control a person.
Problems arise and the individual chooses to stew, fret, and

worry until he gets pain in his neck and down his back. It was not hard work that caused the pain, it was the way he reacted to the problems.

The next time something comes up that bothers you, stop what you are doing and pray quietly, "Lord, I remove all thoughts and agitations from my mind. I do not know all the answers to this problem, but you do. Now Lord, as I cleanse my mind from all pre-conceived ideas, I ask for you to give me the inspiration and an answer to this problem. Direct my thoughts what to do, even now, Lord Jesus. I praise and worship you for helping me in this difficult situation, for you are in control. Thank you, Jesus. Amen."

Then keep your eyes closed, sit quietly and wait for His guidance and direction. If you are desperate and do not want interruptions during this time, take the phone off the hook and lock your door. It is important to wait quietly on the Lord.

The words of old, "Be still, and know that I am God..." (Psalm 46:10), are still true today. It is good to sit still, do nothing, listen and be quiet. It is hard for some people to be quiet, but the blessings of quietness are many.

Instead of ranting and raving, be quiet. Why let your mind sizzle and fry when you can give your vexations to Jesus, who has promised to help you in all things. When He is involved, everything is going to turn out alright; He will keep you safe through it all.

The Lord is thy keeper: the Lord is thy shade upon thy right hand. The sun shall not smite thee by day, nor the moon by night. The Lord shall preserve thee from all evil: he shall preserve thy soul. The Lord shall preserve thy going out and thy coming in from this time forth, and even for evermore (Psalm 121:5-8).

There is no need to get uptight, for this too shall pass! Nothing lasts forever.

Let nothing disturb thee,
Nothing affright thee,
All things are passing;
God never changeth;

Patient endurance
Attaineth to all things;
Who God possesseth
In nothing is wanting;
Alone God sufficeth. [1]

What does anxiety or the state of weariness do? It does not help tomorrow; it only empties today of its strength. It does not help you escape it, it only makes you unfit to cope with it. Give the thing that causes you weariness unto the Lord. David said, "Cast thy burden upon the Lord, and he shall sustain thee" (Psalm 55:22). The following poem expresses it beautifully:

Child of my love, Lean Hard,
And let Me feel the pressure of thy care,
I know thy burden, child, I shaped it;
Poised it in Mine own hand: made no proportion
In its weight to thine unaided strength.
For even as I laid it on I said,
"I shall be near, and while she leans on Me,
This burden shall be Mine, not hers;
So shall I keep My child within the circling arms
Of my own love." Here lay it down nor fear
To impose it on a shoulder upholds

The government of worlds. Yet closer come.
Thou are not near enough. I would embrace thy care
So I might feel My child reposing on My breast.
Thou lovest Me? I knew it. Doubt not then;
But, loving Me, Lean Hard.

Author unknown [2]

You are not asked to stand strong by yourself. You are only asked to be strong in the Lord. You must learn to not lean unto your own strength, but lean on the Lord.

In 1929, J.C. Penney's business was very unstable and he began to worry so much that he lost sleep over it and developed a case of painful shingles. Doctors gave him medicine to tranquilize him, but he still worried about the business.

One night he felt he would die before morning, and so he started writing farewells to his wife, son and friends. The next morning while lying in the bed, he heard singing from the hospital chapel next door, *"No matter what may be the test, God will take care of you...."*

Suddenly he sat up, thinking about God's love. In no time, he had jumped out of bed and entered the chapel, and a miracle took place in his mind and soul. From that day forward, he was released into a feeling of peace knowing that God would take care of him. It worked! Look around you: J.C. Penney stores are in every major city today.

A Chicago physician reports that he had to abandon the use of dogs in an ulcer research program. The dogs refused to get tense and worry, and worry and tension are prominently listed as suspected causes of ulcers.

It was discovered that if you inflict an ulcer upon a dog by artificial methods, he will sit down and placidly cure himself by refusing to be bothered about anything. Maybe that is what you need to do: refuse to be bothered about anything. How? Isaiah tells how.

> He giveth power to the faint; and to them that have no might he increaseth strength. Even the youths shall faint and be weary, and the young men shall utterly fall: *But* they that wait upon the Lord shall renew their strength; they shall mount up with wings as eagles; they shall run, and not be weary; and they shall walk, and not faint (Isaiah 40:29-31).

Waiting is spending time in the Lord's presence. Waiting is trusting the God of glory to give you strength for the journey. His grace is sufficient for all situations. His strength is made strong when you feel like you cannot go any further. When troubles come that would gnaw at the soul, and situations occur that are not to your liking, that is the time to realize that there is a reason for the stops and delays in a person's life. They are not to vex; they are just a part of life that can be used to enrich the soul.

Mrs. Charles Cowman, the writer, shares the following:

> There is no music in a rest, but there is the making of music in it. In our whole life-melody the music is broken off here and there by "rests," and we foolishly think we have come to the end of the tune. God allows a time of forced leisure, sickness, disappointed plans, and frustrated efforts to come, and makes a sudden pause in the choral hymn of our lives; and we lament that our voices must be silent, and our part missing in the music which ever goes up to the ear of the Creator. How does the musician read the "rest"? See him beat the time with unvarying count, and catch up the next note true and steady, as if no breaking place had come in between.

Not without design does God write the music of our lives. Be it ours to learn the tune, and not be dismayed at the "rest." They are not to be slurred over, not to be omitted, not to destroy the melody, not to change the keynote. If we sadly say to ourselves, "There is no music in a 'rest,'" let us not forget "there is the making of music in it." [3]

So when delays come, or "rests" are forced upon you, fret not yourself, but learn something from them. In spite of everything, learn to rest in the Lord, for He cares for you and is not forgetful of you. Whatever touches your heart and is important to you touches the heart of God, for He is as a father to His children. He waits even now for you to go sit close to Him. As you lean against Him and feel the quiet measured beat of His heart, you will be assured that all is well!

"Come ye yourselves apart, and rest awhile,"
Weary, I know it, of the press and throng;
Wipe from thy brow the sweat of dust and toil,
And in my quiet strength again be strong.

Come, tell me all that ye have said and done,
Your victories and failures, hopes and fears,
I know how hardy souls are wooed and won,
My choicest wreathes are always wet with tears.

Come ye, and rest; the journey is too great,
And ye shall faint beside the way, and sink;
The bread of life is here for you to eat,
And here for the wine of love for drink.

Then fresh from converse with your Lord return,

And work till daylight softens into even;
The brief hours are not lost in which ye learn
More of your Master and his rest in Heaven. [3]

Words spoken 2,000 years ago by Jesus Christ still ring with truth and conviction through the airwaves today: "Come unto me, all ye that labour and are heavy laden, and I will give you rest. Take my yoke upon you, and learn of me; for I am meek and lowly in heart: and ye shall find rest unto your souls. For my yoke is easy, and my burden is light" (Matthew 11:28-30).

"Adopt the pace of nature, her secret is patience."

Ralph Waldo Emerson

11

Run With Patience

"In your patience possess ye your soul" (Luke 21:19)

Psychologists list two contributing causes to anxiety: (1) Rush sickness—trying to cram thirty hours of activities into a 24-hour day, and (2) Straining—not getting ahead as fast as you think you should and straining harder for both it and social approval.

When you run according to the anxiety time clock, you will grow weary, but if you are in tune with the Master, walking according to His time schedule and His orders, then you will remain refreshed. Are you rushing madly about, straining to get ahead without taking time to set your clock by His clock? Waiting on God is sometimes the hardest thing to do, but it is the most rewarding thing you can do. It helps you to walk in peace and contentment even when your dreams are unfulfilled. They may be unfulfilled, but they can be yet alive. Work hard, but do not become full of worry and anxiety; just let life flow.

LEARN TO WAIT

Learn to wait—life's hardest lesson,
Learned, perchance, through blinding tears

While the heart-throbs, sadly march
To the tread of passing years.

Constant sunshine, however welcome,
Ne'er would ripen fruit or flower;
Giant oaks owe half their greatness
To the scathing tempest's power.

Human strength and human greatness
Spring not from life's sunny side;
Heroes must be more than driftwood
Floating on a waveless tide.

Anonymous [1]

"...Run with patience, the race that is set before us, Looking unto Jesus the author and finisher of our faith..." (Hebrews 12:1-2). How can you run and be patient at the same time? What is patience? To be *patient* means "to bear or endure pains, trials and hardship without complaint; expectant with calmness or without discontent; also, undisturbed by obstacles, delays, failures, etc.; persevering."

Benjamin Franklin wisely said, "He that can have patience can have what he will." Emerson, the philosopher, wrote, "A man is a hero, not because he is braver than anyone else, but because he is brave for ten minutes longer."

How many masterpieces have been thrown aside for a lack of patience? How many great things were never brought to fruition because of impatience? If you do not feel like doing what you are doing right now, be patient, which is to expect greater things than are happening right now, with a sense of peace. The goal is greater than the pain.

There is a modern painting by Shields which symbolizes the qualities of patience. A being with great strong wings is represented as standing with ankles chained to a sundial. She possesses powers of flight, but these she cannot use until God's appointed time comes.

Meanwhile she waits, crowned with thorns, encircled with briers and brambles—briers which put forth fresh green shoots, which speak of increasing troubles. But she clasps to her breast the Word of God. She bears on her shoulders the yoke of Christ. Her lips are closed uncomplainingly; her eyes are looking forward to things afar. So she waits in faith, knowing that in God's good time the call will come, the fetters be struck from her, and her wings given opportunity to soar. [2]

So work and wait, reaching toward. Thomas Edison said it this way: "Everything comes to him who hustles while he waits." Do not wait and idle away precious time, but wait in expectancy without despair, complaining, or fretfulness, while working and running toward the goal. It will come sure as the sun rises. Every act begets another act; everything that is invested will produce a dividend.

A seed holds within it the potential of reproducing itself again in multiple growth, but it does not reach this potential until it falls into the ground and dies. Every man and woman holds within them a seed of greatness that has the potential to bless another life. But that seed has to endure hardness, pain, and even death to the robbers of that potential, which are laziness, selfishness, and a lack of patience.

Some things you just cannot rush; they demand patience. Weariness and frustration are often the result of a lack of patience. In order to get rid of blahs and weariness, focus your eyes on the goal, work toward it without complaining, and eventually you will get to where you are going. There is nothing that saps strength like a rushed, hurried spirit, complaining all the way about "not enough time to do this, not enough time to do that, I never can get ahead because of too much to do." The problem could stem from being just too impatient and unorganized.

Everyone receives a gift of time every day. Your account is filled with 24 precious hours, and many of them are lost because of poor time management. A master plan is good for a year and even a month, but how each day is handled is the important thing, for days make months, and months make years. Thomas Carlyle wrote, "Our main business is not to see what lies dimly at a distance, but to do what lies clearly at hand." Plan for the future, but give your energy to living each DAY well. If today is lived well, then tomorrow will take care of itself.

Dr. James Gordon Gilkey gave a talk called, "Gaining Emotional Poise" that was later published in *Best Sermons, 1944 Selection,* and subsequently was quoted in *Reader's Digest.* A portion of the sermon was:

Most of us think of ourselves as standing wearily and helplessly at the center of a circle bristling with tasks, burdens, problems, annoyances, and responsibilities which are rushing in upon us. At every moment we have a dozen different things to do, a dozen problems to solve, a dozen strains to endure. We see ourselves as overdriven, overburdened, overtired. This is a common mental picture —and it is totally false. No one of us, however crowded his life, has such an existence.

What is the true picture of your life? Imagine that there is an hourglass on your desk. Connecting the bowl at the top with the bowl at the bottom is a tube so thin that only one grain of sand can pass through it at a time. That is the

Joy Haney / What Do You Do...?

true picture of your life, even on a super-busy day. The crowded hours come to you always one moment at a time. That is the only way they can come. The day may bring many tasks, many problems, strains, but invariably they come in single file. You want to gain emotional poise? Remember the hourglass, the grains of sand dropping one by one.... [3]

Live each minute with patience, without complaint, and you will have lived a day well-spent in your lifelong race toward the goal.

If you have lived well and worked toward an honorable purpose, yet in looking back feel like your dreams have not been fulfilled, do not despair. This is the beauty of the whole scenario; one plants, another waters, but God gives the increase. Your work may not be as spectacular as you would so desire, but you are linked with each human soul, and each adds to the other. What you do builds a bridge for those following behind you. Your work is not wasted as portrayed in the poem entitled, *The Bridge Builder:*

An old man, going a lone highway,
Came at the evening, cold and gray,
To a chasm, vast and deep and wide,
Through which was flowing a sullen tide,
The old man crossed in the twilight dim—
That sullen stream had no fears for him;
But he turned, when he reached the other side,
And built a bridge to span the tide.

"Old man," said a fellow pilgrim near,
"You are wasting strength in building here.
Your journey will end with the ending day:

You never again must pass this way.
You have crossed the chasm, deep and wide,
Why build you the bridge at the eventide?"

The builder lifted his old gray head.
"Good friend, in the path I have come," he said,
"There followeth after me today
A youth whose feet must pass this way.
This chasm that has been naught to me
To that fair-haired youth may a pitfall be.
He, too, must cross in the twilight dim;
Good friend, I am building the bridge for him."

Will Allen Dromcoole [4]

One generation builds a bridge for the next generation.
Building a bridge means helping your neighbor. Jesus said the
second greatest commandment was loving your neighbor as
yourself. You never waste time helping others! When others
do not appreciate what you have been called to do, or question
your motives, wondering why you are doing what you are doing
when they think you should be doing something else, give heed
to the higher call. If you have done a job well and there is no
crowd to applaud you, as others are applauded, and you ponder
the injustice of it all, remember you have done what the Master
asked you to do, and He is the one keeping the books. He will
repay in due time if you do not faint and give up for lack of
applause. The key is to run your appointed race, the course He
sets out for you, with patient endurance, giving your best to
whatever it is, whether it is considered small or great. He alone
is the judge of all things.

Never forget! He is the author and the finisher of your
faith. His spirit will pulsate through every breath you breathe

and accompany you with every step you take. Jesus is the reason for all this! He wants you to make it. He and heaven's angels are cheering you on. If God be for you who can be against you?

*"Great minds have purposes, others
have wishes."*
                    Washington Irving

12

Live With Purpose

"To every thing there is a season, and a time to every purpose under the heaven" (Ecclesiastes 3:1)

A friend once visited Liszt, the composer, at his home in Weimar. When it was time to leave, Liszt offered to accompany his friend to the station, and they set off although the skies looked threatening. Halfway to their destination, a terrible storm erupted causing a tremendous downpour of rain. Liszt continued to talk about a new composition he was working on.

Finally the friend asked him why the storm did not bother him. Liszt answered, "I never take notice of that which takes no notice of me."

In other words, his purpose, or the thing that consumed his thinking, absorbed his attention more than the storm. He did not even notice that which threatened to disturb most people. His emphasis was on a dream that was becoming a reality more than the circumstances that surrounded him.

To overcome weariness, it is essential to refocus on the purpose for which we are destined. When you know where you are going and are determined to get there, virtually nothing will detain you or keep you from reaching your goal, except God, of course. Turbulent situations, difficulties, and times of weariness only serve as a basis for improvement for those that have a burning desire to succeed.

F.B. Meyer once said, "Difficulties are absolutely nothing to the man who knows that he is on the mission on which God has sent him. They are only opportunities for him to show his power; problems to manifest his skill in their solution; thunder-clouds on which to paint the frescoes of his unrealized tenderness." [1]

You need to know where you are going! Life without a mission is miserable. A life that is aimless is both restless and forceless. Purpose should guide you. Your days must be charted. It is useless to just exist day by day. What are you living for? What is your purpose?

Lyman Abbott, D.D. says,

> I pluck an acorn from the greensward, and hold it to my ear; and this is what it says to me: "By and by the birds will come and rest in me. By and by I will furnish shade for the cattle. By and by I will provide warmth for the home in the pleasant fire. By and by I will be shelter from the storm to those who have gone under the roof. By and by I will be the strong ribs of the great vessel, and the tempest will beat against me in vain while I carry men across the Atlantic."
>
> "O foolish little acorn, wilt thou be all this?" I ask.
>
> And the acorn answers, *"Yes, God and I."* [2]

The acorn lived not only for the moment. Even in the days when he grew weary of the winds and storms, his purpose kept him going. Plod if you must, but keep your purpose in mind. It will take you over mine-fields and through swollen rivers, keep you in fiery furnaces and many other life-threatening events. It

Joy Haney / What Do You Do...?

does not matter what experiences a person is asked to go through, it matters that the purpose is kept in focus.

Something wonderful happens when a person decides that he will let his purposes run parallel to the purposes of God. He comes in to abide and guide when there is an alignment with His greater plans. Acquaintance with Him grows, ripens and unfolds into continual fellowship. The human spirit should be a cathedral where God reigns and fills the soul and its aspirations.

An unknown author wrote these powerful words:

If we are not certain, it may be because we are living at too low a level. If we live for pleasure or for money or for fame, then the spiritual realities must of necessity become nebulous and vague. To feel that we are immortal we must live like immortals. Gazing constantly into the trivial blinds the eyes to the splendor of the eternal, and working always for fading wealth robs the heart of its belief in the crown of glory. God breathes assurance only into hearts which are open to Him. To those who give themselves whole-heartedly to the service of mankind in the spirit of his Son, He communicates not only peace and joy, but an unconquerable conviction that when work here is finished, to die is gain. [3]

Paul said it! "I have fought a good fight, I have finished my course, I have kept the faith; Henceforth there is laid up for me a crown of righteousness, which the Lord, the righteous judge, shall give me at that day; and not to me only, but unto all them also that love his appearing" (II Timothy 4:7-8).

He was not beating the air; he had purpose, a course to follow. He was coming to the end of his course and was delighted that the purpose of life that had guided him had not been in vain. He did not emphasize his weariness and trials as he neared his homecoming. Instead he emphasized what he had lived for since his original purpose had been changed by God Himself on the road to Damascus.

The important thing to consider here is, not only did Paul have a purpose, but he successfully activated it. To purpose is not enough; although it is necessary and grand to have direction, it must be carried through. Someone said, *"Purposes, like eggs, unless they be hatched into action, will run into decay."*

DON'T QUIT
When things go wrong, as they sometimes will,
When the road you're trudging seems all uphill,
When the funds are low and the debts are high,
And you want to smile, but you have to sigh,
When care is pressing you down a bit,
Rest, if you must—but don't you quit.

Life is queer with its twists and turns,
As everyone of us sometimes learns,
And many a failure turns about
When he might have won had he stuck it out;
Don't give up, though the pace seems slow—
You might succeed with another blow.

Often the goal is nearer than
It seems to a faint and faltering man,
Often the struggler has given up
When he might have captured the victor's cup.
And he learned too late, when the night slipped down,
How close he was to the golden crown.

Success is failure turned inside out—

The silver tint of the clouds of doubt—
And you never can tell how close you are,
It may be near when it seems afar;
So stick to the fight when you're hardest hit—
It's when things seem worst that you mustn't quit.

Author unknown [4]

How can you quit if you have a driving force? A person without purpose or goals is only a shell of the person that God intended him to be. *Mere existence is misery.* If you have never struggled and won, you have never lived, for the exuberant joy of a conqueror is indescribable.

Those who merely exist with no purpose to help others, die with their music and potential inside of them. A coward who is afraid to face life head-on, to purpose, plan, fight and win will die many times. Those who live for nothing, only to eat, sleep, shop, go to work, and then start all over again live in a private hell of desperation. An endless cycle of life that is molded only by the demand for the bare necessities of life becomes a prison.

It is time to break out of the dank prison with its stale air that is slowly snuffing out your dreams. Now is the time to let the breath of purpose and inspiration blow through your heart and mind. You are one step away from eternity, the place where spirits dwell. What are you doing with your spirit? How are you affecting the hearts and spirits of other men and women?

Is it possible to daily live in a box of unconcern when so many are hurting? Have you taken the time to lift someone up today, or are you locked into your own prison of despair? Can you see the load on the other man's back, or are you blinded to it because of your own pre-occupation with self? What are you doing to help the Lord Jesus on earth? What is your purpose in life? It is better to fight for something than to die for nothing.

One might argue, "All I have time for is just getting by. By the time I go to work and do everything that is essential to live, there is not much time left." You can stay in that vein of thought or you can let a light shine into the dark recesses in your mind. You can do anything you want to do, if you want to badly enough! This is where purposes and priorities come into focus. You must plan your work, and then work your plan.

Look at the host of men and women who made great contributions to mankind. They were normal flesh and blood, but they marched to a different drummer than the normal person. Their heartstrings were being played by purpose, need, desire, and grit. Excuses were not in the song they sang, but purpose and plan made up the refrain. The music of passion for a certain cause blinded their eyes to impossibilities and the prolonged pause. They did not wait forever and ever, but plunged right in, pushing every available lever. They did not look at what could not be done, they looked at what could be done.

If someone asked, "Do you have time?", they just said, "I'll make time." Desire and purpose put fire in their brain as they walked life's road facing obstacles and pain. The enemy could not stop them, for the fire of inspiration was bubbling to the brim. They did not walk alone, for as they passed wrecked lives along the way, their hand was extended in love as they scattered sun rays—rays of hope, faith, and love—to each one they cared for and each one they touched.

The purpose that becomes part of the sinewy tissues of the heart, and lodges in the soul of mankind is as vital as breathing, for it is the pulsating reason for true life. It is giving back to God and others what He has given to you. So why let temporary weariness steal away a dream or purpose? Fight for it, for you are fighting for your very life. When you cease both to dream and have purpose, you die. Do not refuse to take advantage of the opportunities to enrich the lives of others that life gives you. On this your purpose must rest: bringing God closer to the heart of another.

Refuse to open your purse, and soon you cannot open your sympathy. Refuse to give, and soon you will cease to enjoy that which you have. Refuse to love, and you lose the power to love and be loved. Withhold your affections and you become a moral paralytic. But the moment you open wider the door of your life, you let the sunshine of your life into some soul. [5]

Do not let past performances or failures sink your heart and soul into the abyss of regrets, thinking that all is lost. This is the beginning of a new day. Listen to Christ, not your flesh or the devil. He said if you are in Him, things become new. "Therefore, if any man be in Christ, he is a new creature: old things are passed away; behold, all things are become new" (II Corinthians 5:17). It is time to get a fresh touch from Him and let the breath of heaven's inspiration blow through your heart, soul, and mind. Let it blow all the stale air and thoughts of, "I can't" and "Life's a drag" out of your heart!

It has often been said that opportunities come but once, but that is not true. Walter Malone shares his insight on that in the poem called *Opportunity:*

They do me wrong who say I come no more
When once I knock and fail to find you in,
For every day I stand outside your door
And bid you wake, and rise to fight and win. [5]

Opportunity stares you in the face every day that you live. Some people only dream that if they had the proper tools, they would get the job done, but others look not upon the propriety of things; the need becomes greater than perfect situations. Things will never be perfect, so you may as well dig in where you are and get started. Are you waiting for that golden moment to transpire? You will wait forever! In the trenches, grubby and dirty, and in hard work, arduous and difficult, opportunity lies hidden and waits, so grab it and go with it.

This I beheld, or dreamed it in a dream:
There spread a cloud of dust along a plain;
And underneath the cloud, or in it, raged
A furious battle, and men yelled, and swords
Shocked upon swords and shields. A prince's banner
Wavered, then staggered backward, hemmed by foes.
A craven hung along the battle's edge
And thought, "Had I a sword of keener steel—
That blue blade that the king's son bears—but this
Blunt thing—!" He snapt and flung it from his hand,
And, lowering, crept away and left the field.
Then came the king's son, wounded, sore bestead,
And weaponless, and saw the broken sword,
Hilt-buried in the dry and trodden sand,
And ran and snatched it, and with battle-shout
Lifted afresh, he hewed his enemy down,
And saved a great cause that heroic day.

Edward Rowland Sill [6]

You can make excuses why it cannot be done, and someone else will come along and do it. If you dream it, God will help you do it. Wait not for another day! This is the day to begin, to purpose and plan. If God be for you, who or what can be against you? In your planning, remember who your partner is.

That is what saved Zerubbabel and the children of Israel. As they were building again the house of the Lord at Jerusalem, the enemy came against them and tried to stop them. "And hired counsellors against them, to frustrate their PURPOSE..." (Ezra 4:5). The next thing the enemy did was write to King Artaxerxes and ask for his help in stopping the people from building.

It worked! The king sent out a letter unto the Jews at Jerusalem and "...made them to cease by force and power. Then ceased the work of the house of God which is at Jerusalem..." (Ezra 4:23-24). Did this stop the Jews? No, after awhile they just started building the house of the Lord again, and messengers came asking them, "Who hath commanded you to build this house, and to make up this wall?" (Ezra 5:3).

King Darius came into the picture. They appealed to him and he searched for the scrolls and found old promises that had never been fulfilled in the lives of the children of Israel. So he favored God's people and said, "Let the work of this house of God alone" (Ezra 6:7). The end result? "And they builded, and finished it, according to the commandment of the God of Israel" (Ezra 6:14).

Every person that tries to do anything worthwhile is going to have those that try to frustrate the purpose. Make up your mind to never quit. If it was worth starting, it is worth finishing. It does not matter whether you feel like it or not, just do it! I am convinced that Zerubbabel and all the Jews did not enjoy the wrangling and the delays that accompanied that which they were responsible to do.

There is an interesting passage that paints a vivid picture of their enthusiasm at the beginning of the project. During the time of the coming to Jerusalem after their captivity, they planned the building of the walls, meeting together in one great service. They sang, praised God and gave thanks unto the Lord for His mercy. What was the climate of the meeting?

And all the people shouted with a great shout, when they praised the Lord, because the foundation of the house of the Lord was laid. But many of the priests and Levites and chief of the fathers, who were ancient men, that had seen the first house, when the foundation of this house was laid before their eyes, wept with a loud voice; and many shouted aloud for joy: So that the people could not discern the noise of the shout of joy from the noise of the weeping of the people: for the people shouted with a loud shout, and the noise was heard afar off (Ezra 3:11-14).

It went from shout, to opposition, to total shut-down, then back to the project, on to the finish, and then to joy. They felt like shouting in the beginning, and shouted so loud they could be heard for miles. Then after the initial shout, the trials, opposition, and weariness came. After the conquering they felt like singing again, just as every conqueror feels!

Joy Haney / What Do You Do...?

"It seems to me we can never give up longing and wishing while we are thoroughly alive. There are certain things we feel to be beautiful and good, and we must hunger after them."

George Eliot

13

Get Motivated

"And whatsoever ye do, do it heartily" (Colossians 3:23)

When you are excited or motivated about something, it is almost virtually impossible to become weary in your mind. Motivation gives you the power or the juice to do things that others consider impossible.

Boddy Dodd, Georgia Tech's athletic director, tells of the football coach who, with his team leading 7-6 in the last minute of play, carefully instructed his quarterback not to pass under any condition. But when the ball was carried within the opponent's ten-yard line, the temptation overcame the quarterback to pass. His pass was intercepted by the rival's fastest back, who broke into an open field and raced toward pay dirt. He was speeding past midfield when suddenly, out of nowhere, the quarterback who had passed overtook him and brought him down.

After the game, the losing coach remarked to his barely victorious counterpart, "I'll never understand how your boy overtook my fastest back."

"Well, I'll tell you," came the reply. "Your back was running for a touchdown; my boy was running for his life."

It depends what you are running for in life. Your degree of weariness will either go up or down by what motivates you. It is time to get motivated, so that the things that would bother you normally are not able to bother you at all. As you get on fire with a purpose, your body produces extra energy and adrenalin, making it possible to do things that surprise those around you as well as yourself.

In Bible times, during a fierce battle, one of David's mighty men, Eleazar, the son of Dodo, did a mighty feat which surprised those around him. "He arose, and smote the Philistines until his hand was weary, and his hand clave unto the sword; and the Lord wrought a great victory that day" (II Samuel 23:10). Because of his motivating force he slew several hundred men.

The church of the nineties must be motivated to fight until her hand cleaves unto the sword, and the Lord will bring about a great victory. She will be surprised of the strength that will flow through her as she becomes motivated by the will and purpose of God. The church does not need as much sleep as she thinks she needs. She needs to ignite with fire until the whole world can feel her fire of truth and evangelism.

Thomas Edison was so on fire with his desire to invent a light bulb that he was able to work twenty hours and sleep only four. He was not bogged down with resentment, anger, boredom, and all the other negative emotions that take away proper motivation. He lived in such a state of excitement that it actually gave him a sense of euphoria.

Dr. Ernest Hartmann of Boston reports that people who worry need more sleep than those who push problems aside and get on with the job. He deduced from his studies that those who need more than nine hours of sleep every night are worriers who apparently mull over their problems while they dream. The long sleepers in his study spend two or three times as long in rapid eye movement or "rem" sleep, the period when dreams occur. He speculated they need the extra dreaming to resolve mental and emotional needs.

It is apparent that Edison was not a worrier; had he been it would have slowed down his progress and taken the joy and excitement out of his task. He was one that was able to sleep peacefully when it was time to sleep.

Motivation takes away fears and the thoughts of, "Maybe I can't do this." When a person is motivated he thinks only of accomplishing his purpose and does not even give a thought to whether he will do it or not. His excitement and inner confidence—that glow of motivation—carries him to the finish line.

There is something about motivation and fire within a person that has amazed people down through the centuries. Stories in newspapers and periodicals have often related incidents of heroic deeds such as a 200-pound man lifting a Volkswagen all by himself when it means saving his little girl's life. Many stories attest to the fact that, when people are motivated, they can pull from sources they are not aware of .

Mrs. Julia Adams had been a hopeless invalid for nine years, and for six of them she had lain in bed, as helpless as an infant. But one day she walked proudly into Jefferson Market police court and gave evidence that would help convict two men who were the unconscious instruments of her restoration.

The excitement of hearing noises in the night, of the house being aroused, and of the discovery that house-breakers had removed $800 worth of silver, worked on her feelings so powerfully that she amazed her family by getting out of bed and walking about the house like one of them.

You can do more than you think you can if the motivation is there. It releases you into a new dimension of excitement. A person who is motivated does not think about the drudgery connected with the work. He thinks only of getting it done and works feverishly to do it. He does not look at his job with a feeling of dread. His feet are too busy flying trying to accomplish it.

There are little things that prove this point. Many a dirty house has been cleaned quickly when the woman of the house learned that her mother-in-law was coming over unexpectedly. Let someone who is tired and about ready to fall over from exhaustion receive an invitation that involves extra money or a fulfillment of a special dream of his, and see how alive he becomes. It is all in motivation.

People are motivated by different things: anger, competition, poverty, desperation, daily associations, love, as well as other things. Most everyone can be motivated to do something that is distasteful, full of hard work, or extremely difficult if properly motivated.

If you get someone mad enough by suggesting that he is unable to do something, many times he will respond in his mind, "I'll show you." Then he will work until he does it.

Such was the case of a young college boy who desired to teach a Sunday School class and proceeded to ask for one. The director gave him the class but told him it would be a difficult one as the children involved were from unstable homes.

As the young man worked at his class, seemingly he was unable to keep a good attendance record for any of the boys in his class except one. Finally in discouragement he went to the director and told him of his decision to quit. The director looked at him and said, "You're worthless! Everyone of you college students want to do something great for God, but you cannot even teach a difficult Sunday School class successfully." The young college student got so mad that he told the director he would try it again. This time, motivated by the director's nettling words, he succeeded. He took one boy and built his class up to 55 in attendance; he even got some of the parents to come to church.

Motivation comes in many ways. Sometimes adversity causes a person to excel and do things that are difficult; whereas, the same person without adversity might just settle down to being normal. Such was the case of a suffering soldier told about in a Greek story. He had a disease that was extremely painful and could at any time destroy his life. In every campaign he was in the forefront of the hottest battle. His pain prompted him to fight without worrying about death, and because he knew he could die anytime, he took dares that other men would be afraid to take.

His general, Antigonus, admired the man's bravery and was so impressed with his great skills as a warrior that he had a renowned physician work with the soldier until he was cured. Something happened from that day forward. No longer was he seen at the front. He avoided danger instead of seeking it and sought to protect his life instead of risking it. Whereas the struggle with his disease caused him to fight well, his health and comfort destroyed his usefulness as a soldier. So it is that sometimes people do things as a result of adversity that they would not do if all were going well.

Desperation will cause a person to do things that he would not do under normal conditions. The story is told of a young man years ago from Stanford University seeking part-time employment, who stood before Louis Janin. "All I need right now," said Mr. Janin, "is a stenographer."

"I'll take the job, but I cannot start until next Tuesday," said the eager young man.

On Tuesday when the young man showed up for work, Mr. Janin asked him why he could not start to work until now. The answer surprised the employer: "Because I had to rent a typewriter and learn to use it." The zealous typist was Herbert

Hoover. Some people are motivated simply because of a desperate need.

There are others that are motivated by poverty. When Sherwood Anderson was beginning his writing career, his publisher thought that he would encourage him by sending him each Friday a check big enough to meet his week's expenses. Mr. Anderson received the check for three weeks, then went to his publisher's office and said, "It's no use. I find it impossible to write with security staring me in the face."

So it is, people are motivated by different things, but everyone is motivated partially by the things that surround them. Such was the case of a missionary that went to Japan. Before going he told the board his reason for going: "Woe is me if I preach not the Gospel to the brethren."

Immediately his friend stood up and remarked, "I know why he feels so compelled to go. He sleeps under a missionary chart on which there are 856 black squares representing 856 million heathen, and 200 million Mohammedans. Any man sleeping under such a chart must decide to become a foreign missionary or have a nightmare every night in the week."

If you want something bad enough, you usually will acquire it. If you need motivation, and want it desperately enough, you will find a way to get it. No one will have to ram it down your throat or force you to find it. You will either read a book, view a panorama, fall in love, or reach until you grasp hold of your goal.

There was once a young man that went to Socrates one day and asked him for wisdom and learning. Socrates simply told the young man to follow him. He led the way down to the seashore. They then waded out into the water up to their chests, and Socrates grabbed the young man and held his head under water despite his struggles.

Joy Haney / What Do You Do...?

Finally, when most of his resistance was gone, Socrates lifted him up and laid him on the beach and returned to his location in the marketplace. When the young man regained his strength, he went to look for Socrates. Upon finding him, the young man asked the reason for his strange behavior.

Socrates asked him a question. "When you were under water, what did you want more than anything?"

The boy replied, "I wanted air."

Socrates then said, "When you want knowledge and understanding as badly as you wanted air, you will not have to ask anyone to give it to you."

When you want something bad enough, you are going to find it. That is why difficulties, desperation and struggles are oft times hidden blessings. They make one perform as if his life depended upon it.

Different things motivate different people, but the greatest motivation is *love*. Paul said, "For the love of Christ constraineth us" (II Corinthians 5:14). That is how he shook a world. It was love that carried him through beatings, prisons, false accusations, and shipwrecks. Paul just kept going; he never gave up. He affected a world for the gospel's sake like no other man.

Everyone can be motivated and when they are motivated— look out, world—nothing can stop them. They will even forget to eat, schedules will go out the door, and the thing for which they are motivated will take pre-eminence in their life.

Such was the case when an American visited a small English town and lost his valuable dog. He asked to have a notice printed in the local evening paper offering $100.00 for its return. Evening came, but no paper appeared.

The impatient American paced up and down waiting for the paper. When it did not come, he walked down to the newspaper office and found only the night watchman on duty. He asked him, "Isn't the paper coming out?"

The watchman replied, "I doubt it, sir. The whole staff is out looking for a lost dog."

The entire staff was motivated not by a desire to help the distraught American, but by a desire to acquire money. The promise of money is a motivation that works with most people. Why do people go broke playing the lottery, gambling away their hard-earned paycheck, or investing in a cause? It is the promise of more money.

I will never forget a minister named Winifred Black. He came to hold a Sunday School promotion at the church where my husband is pastor. Being a great promoter he inspired enthusiasm in everyone to go out and bring people to Sunday School. When Sunday morning arrived, there was Reverend Black with about fifteen kids lined up on the front pew of the church. He brought more than anyone else.

When asked how he did it, he replied, "I promised a silver dollar to everyone that came." He then held up a silver dollar, flipped it in the air and said with a smile, "It works every time."

If you have lost your motivation, if you dread doing what you are doing, and life has become a drudge, you are beginning to slowly die. So what does a dying man wisely do? He seeks to get back that which ignites or motivates him. Do something to motivate yourself, but do it quickly: take a break, read a book, pray, surround yourself with inspirational things. Oh, there are so many things to motivate you. It is impossible to name them all. The main thing is to come alive! Do not stay in the rut you are in! As Ralph Waldo Emerson said, "Nothing great was ever achieved without enthusiasm."

In his book, *How I Raised Myself From Failure to Success in Selling,* Frank Bettger tells about when he was a young man playing baseball in Johnstown, Pennsylvania, in the Tri-State

League and was fired. Instead of walking off the field with a grudge against the coach, he went to him and asked why he was fired. The manager said he fired him because he was lazy. That was the last thing Frank expected to hear.

"You drag yourself around the field like a veteran who has been playing ball for twenty years," the coach said.

Frank answered, "Well, Bert, I'm so nervous, so scared, that I want to hide my fear from the crowd, and especially from the other players on the team. Besides, I hope that by taking it easy, I'll get rid of my nervousness."

"Frank," he said, "it will never work. That's the thing that is holding you down. Whatever you do after you leave, for heaven's sake, wake yourself up, and put some life and enthusiasm into your work!"

Shortly thereafter, Frank went to play in the New England League. From the minute he appeared on the field he acted like a man electrified. He acted as though he were alive with a million batteries. He threw the ball around the diamond so fast and so hard that it almost knocked the infielders' hands apart. Once, he slid into third base with so much energy and force that the third baseman fumbled the ball and Frank was able to score an important run. Yes, it was all a show, an act he was putting on. Did it work? He said:

It worked like magic. Three things happened.
1. My enthusiasm almost entirely overcame my fear. In fact my nervousness began to work for me, and I played far better than I ever thought I was capable of playing.
2. My enthusiasm affected the other players on the team, and they too became enthusiastic.
3. Instead of dropping with the heat (nearly 100 degrees), I felt better during the game and after it was over than I had ever felt before.

My biggest thrill came the following morning when I read in the New Haven newspaper: "This new player, Bettger, has a barrel of enthusiasm. He inspired our boys. They not only won the game, but looked better than at any time this season." [1]

After he left baseball and got into selling, he started out as a failure. He soon realized that the very thing that had threatened to wreck his playing in baseball was now threatening to wreck his career as a salesman.

Frank Bettger shares how a statement made by Walter P. Chrysler had such an impact on him, that he carried it in his pocket for a week. He read it over forty times until he memorized it. Walter Chrysler, when asked to give the secret of success, listed the various qualities, such as ability, capacity, energy, but added that the real secret was enthusiasm. "Yes, more than enthusiasm," said Chrysler, "I would say excitement. I like to see men get excited. When they get excited, they get customers excited, and we get business." [2]

"Enthusiasm isn't merely an outward expression. Once you begin to acquire it, enthusiasm works constantly within you. You may be sitting quietly in your home...an idea occurs to you...that idea begins to develop...finally, you become consumed with enthusiasm...nothing can stop you." [3]

If Frank became excited over a little round ball thrown through the air, and then later over a product that would eventually wear out, why cannot the church become excited over an eternal truth? Is it not time to let the fire of God's love burn within until the whole world knows about it?

The reason many people are not motivated is because they are too full of self-centeredness. They are constantly looking in the mirror, preening about, and concerned only with presenting a better image. When this happens, there eventually comes a revulsion of self.

> Weary of myself, and sick of asking
> What I am, and what I ought to be,
> I gaze into the heavens and they speak to me.
> "Wouldst thou be as these are? Live as they,
> Unaffrighted by the silence round them,
> Undistracted by the sights they see,
> Bounded by themselves, and unregardful
> In what state God's other works may be.
> In their own tasks all their powers pouring,
> These attain the mighty life you see."
> O, air born voice! long since, severely clear,
> A cry like thine in mine own heart I hear—
> "Resolve to be thyself; and know that he
> Who finds himself loses his misery!"

Matthew Henry [4]

How do you find yourself? Jesus gave the secret to finding yourself when He said, "If any man will come after me, let him deny himself, and take up his cross, and follow me, for whosoever will save his life shall lose it: and whosoever will lose his life for my sake shall *find it*" (Matthew 16:24-25).

It is essential to get lost in a cause bigger than yourself in order to really live. When self is constantly in focus, misery begins. Pampered flesh becomes soft, flabby, and weak. People that are bound up only in themselves are unhappy. Someone asked Socrates why it was that Alcibiades, who was a brilliant and able man and who had traveled so much, seeing much of the world, was nevertheless an unhappy man. Socrates replied, "Because wherever he goes Alcibiades takes himself with him."

Wars are won by men who are not afraid to throw themselves into a cause bigger than themselves, to get out of their self. If you want to win the war against your weariness, do not sit and constantly analyze yourself, although it is good from time to time to look inside yourself and make an evaluation of your inner man, so as to improve what is weak or lacking. But preoccupation with self is not healthy! Jesus said it! What higher authority do you need to be convinced of it?

"Aim at perfection in everything, though in most things it is unattainable. However, they who aim at it, and persevere, will come nearer to it than those whose laziness and despondency make them give it up as unattainable."

Lord Chesterfield

14

Top Performance

"Seek that ye may excel to the edifying of the church"
(I Corinthians 14:12)

Everyone wants to, or should want to, give top performance to whatever they are doing. It should be the desire of all to serve with excellence, but in order to do so there must be guidelines. Many things can be avoided. Weariness can be used to make a situation better, but it should not be a common feeling. This well-known emotion should not become too familiar. Often bad things happen because of disregard to common sense, overloaded circuits, or just plain rebellion to subtle warnings that speak advice. How many times have you felt the warning signs of weariness tugging in your brain, but you just kept on without listening—until you got a bad case of it?

Once a man who was walking along Fourth Avenue in New York stopped on a temporary bridge to watch some work being done on the subway. A workman advised him to move on, as he was liable to get hurt. The man refused, claiming he had a right to be on a public street. A few minutes later he was struck on the head by a piece of iron from a pipe high above. He was severely hurt.

To keep up a top performance and continually give forth the best, one must give heed to the signals of the body and spirit. If you keep on as if everything were alright, sooner or later there will be a crash on the head, for that is where weariness starts: in the mind. It is there where the continual wearing away causes the glow to fade and you are left with drudgery.

Each day a clean sheet of paper is given to everyone. Each person fills the blank sheet with words, deeds, thoughts, and purposes. You can work hard at just getting by, cheating a little here and there, but it is certain, whatever is written on that paper will send things back to you. You receive wages according to what is represented on the paper. You can get more out of life if you put more into it.

MY WAGE

I bargained with Life for a penny,
And life would pay no more,
However, I begged at evening
When I counted my scanty store;

For Life is a just employer,
He gives you what you ask,
But once you have set the wages,
Why, you must bear the task.

I worked for a menial's hire,
Only to learn, dismayed,
That any wage I had asked of Life,
Life would have paid.

Jessie B. Rittenhouse [1]

You determine what you receive by your performance. Will it be mediocrity or will it be excellence? Are you giving your best, or giving just enough to qualify? Do you want to qualify or do you want to win? It is not enough to be in the race, for the race is not the end; it is only the means.

If you want to be miserable, do just enough to get the job done, but not enough to make it shine. If it is worth doing, it is worth doing well. "Half-there" is an open door for weariness. Jesus never did cotton to half-baked efforts. He said, "And thou shalt love the Lord thy God with all thy heart, and with all thy soul, and with all thy mind, and with all thy strength: this is the first commandment" (Mark 12:30).

Throw your heart ahead of you and follow it; do not leave your heart behind. If you are going to get your feet wet, you might as well get in all the way. The wise Solomon said, "Whatsoever thy hand findeth to do, do it with thy might; for there is no work, nor device, nor knowledge, nor wisdom, in the grave, whither thou goest" (Ecclesiastes 9:10).

Do not live as if you were in the grave—dead, dried up, listless and unenthused—while you have breath in your body. If the Word says to do everything with all your might, why settle for less? It is time to come alive to the possibilities around you, giving your best shot to all that you do. Whatever you lack, God will make up the difference, but if you do nothing, God will also reward you, but what a dismal reward.

In Matthew 25, Jesus told a story of how the lord of an estate called his three trusted servants together and told them he was going to be traveling into another country. He gave each of them some money and told them to be good stewards over it. While the lord was gone, the first servant took the money that had been given him and invested it. It was the same with the second servant, but the third hid the money away and did nothing.

Upon the lord's return some time later, he called the three servants together and asked about the money he had given them. The first servant told him he had doubled the money, and the lord commended him; the same with the second servant. The third servant had excuses of why he did not invest the money, and the lord fired him on the spot.

The lord said to each of the two servants who gave their best performance, "Well done, thou good and faithful servant: thou hast been faithful over a few things, I will make thee ruler over many things: enter thou into the joy of thy lord" (Matthew 25:21,23).

To the third servant who had the excuse that he was afraid, the lord simply said,

> Thou wicked and slothful servant, thou knewest that I reap where I sowed not, and gather where I have not strawed: Thou oughtest therefore to have put my money to the exchangers, and then at my coming I should have received mine own with usury. Take therefore the talent from him, and give it unto him which hath ten talents. And cast ye the unprofitable servant into outer darkness: there shall be weeping and gnashing of teeth (Matthew 25:26-28,30).

Would you rather be a little weary in doing, and reap because you fainted not? Or would you rather give in to the pressures, quit, do nothing and have everlasting torment? The Lord God emphasizes profit all through the scriptures: sowing versus slothfulness, reaping versus lack. If you want top performance and want to be rewarded for it, there is hard work involved. Lazy people will never make it. The reward is for the diligent, persevering, and courageous—those who are willing to work or fight until the sword cleaves to the hand, if need be.

There is a stern warning in Isaiah 33 which simply says, "Woe to thee that spoilest, and dealest treacherously...The highways lie waste, the wayfaring man ceaseth: he hath broken the covenant, he hath despised the cities, he regardeth no man" (Verses 1,8).

This is dealing with a particular time of Bible history and prophecy, but the truth is applicable for all. He who spoils away the good things that God has placed in his hand, who deals in a treacherous mannerism, who breaks covenants, and regards no man is a picture of self-will, a lazy spirit, and disrespectful of God or man. The judgment for one like this is bone-chilling.

The good part of this scripture passage is that those that choose to honor God and follow his Word are blessed with honor and victory. The question is asked, "Who among us shall dwell with the devouring fire? who among us shall dwell with everlasting burnings?" (Isaiah 33:14). And he answers it by giving them hope. If one did not waste, spoil, or deal treacherously, then he had blessing promised.

He that walketh righteously, and speaketh uprightly; he that despiseth the gain of oppressions, that shaketh his hands from holding of bribes, that stoppeth his ears from hearing of blood, and shutteth his eyes from seeing evil: He shall dwell on high: his place of defence shall be the munitions of rocks: bread shall be given him; his waters shall be sure. Thine eyes shall see the king in his beauty...The Lord is our king: he will save us (Isaiah 33:15-17,22).

Keep your eyes on the Lord. Keep your hands involved in righteous causes. Keep yourself from becoming involved in gossip and bitter motives. Walk with the fire of love and passion for Jesus Christ in your heart. Give everything you have and you will see the King in His beauty. He will set you on high and He will be your defence.

Top performance—is it worth it? If you could ask Joseph of old who went from the pit to the prison and then to the palace, he would say a big yes! His performance under pressure prepared him for the top position in the entire country.

If you want to rule and reign with the Lord, you must be willing to take some knocks and pain, but get back up with a song in your heart and purpose in your brain. Fix your eyes on the goal, work like you have never worked before, and by God's grace and *your* persistence you are going to make it! Paul said, "...Go on unto perfection..." (Hebrews 6:1). Keep reaching for higher goals and you will keep gaining new heights in God.

Joy Haney / What Do You Do...?

"Some people grumble because God placed thorns among roses; why not thank God for placing roses among thorns?"

Anonymous

15

Attitudes

"Glorify God in your body and spirit" (I Corinthians 6:20)

You are what your attitudes are. They make or break you. An attitude is the spirit of a thing. It gives color, personality, character, and sets the mood for what is being done. You can view an ocean with an attitude of awe and be breathtakingly swept up in the moment of it, or you can look at it with an attitude of skepticism and boredom while missing the whole grandeur of it. You can either regard the church house with respect or treat it with disrespect.

Attitudes are pulsating feelings that surround you every day. While many feel like it is just another day, it is not just another day. Destinies are determined each day, but yet there are those who will choose to talk only about mundane things, though they be on the edge of eternity. You have a choice to look at things through either a temporal eye or eternal one. Your attitude reveals how you face the many difficulties that life brings. Anyway you look at life, it is a risk. The baby could suffocate from crib death. The toddler could fall and hurt itself. The child at school could be kidnapped on the way home. The teenager could die in a school bus wreck. You can either worry, fret and withdraw into safe cocoons because of the risks involved, or you can step out into the sunshine with courage. Courage is the ability to face difficulties with vigor, strength, dignity, firmness and valor. Pertinent questions are asked each person in the form of a poem written by E.V. Cooke, simply entitled *Courage*.

Did you tackle the trouble that came your way
With a resolute heart and cheerful?
Or hide your face from the light of day
With a craven soul and fearful?
O, a trouble's a ton, or a trouble's an ounce,
Or a trouble is what you make it,
And it isn't the fact that you're hurt that counts,
But only how did you take it?
You are beaten to earth? Well, well, what's that?
Come up with a smiling face.
It's nothing against you to fall down flat,
But to lie there—that's disgrace.
The harder you're thrown, why, the higher you bounce;
Be proud of your blackened eye!
It isn't the fact that you're licked that counts;
It's how did you fight—and why? [1]

What kinds of attitudes are you bringing to life? What controls you? What makes you act the way you act? Attitudes definitely affect the emotions. They can cause weariness, tiredness and a bitter feeling towards situations.

It is time to clean the inner house. Throw open the curtains that have shielded the light from shining in and, using the Spirit of God, vacuum everything out that hampers you from operating at your maximum level. In order to operate with enthusiasm and purpose, there must be a cleansing from weights and sins. Sin must be put away. "If I regard iniquity in my heart, the Lord will not hear me," (Psalm 66:18). "But your iniquities have separated between you and your God, and your sins have hid his face from you, that he will not hear," (Isaiah 59:2).

God gives energy, light, inspiration and strength. In order to receive these things, there has to be a cleansing of our inner thoughts, motives and mind. If sin or things that displease God separate us from Him, then that means that we become exhausted mentally, which in turn affects the physical.

A COMPLAINING OR THANKFUL ATTITUDE?

One of the greatest ways to deplete energy is to have a complaining attitude. Henry Van Dyke said, "They who work without complaining do the holy will of God."

Some people grumble because God placed thorns among the roses instead of thanking God for the roses. The habit of grumbling and complaining quickly brings to the grumbler a tired, weary spirit.

Did you know that a great part of the world goes to bed hungry every night? And that many do not know the meaning of the word *home?* That many cannot read or write? That although the Lord Jesus came to earth over 2,000 years ago, over half of the world has never even so much as heard His name?

Some people have so much and yet grumble at a mere inconvenience. What are you tired from? Is it the responsibility of your prosperity? Are you blessed and do not even recognize it? Are you so selfish all you can think about is your aches and pains? Has self-centeredness become your thought pattern?

If so, there needs to be a conscious working at having an uncomplaining attitude in your struggles, to be brave in the battles, and unswerving in your convictions. An uncomplaining attitude will produce iron in your soul, strengthening instead of weakening you.

It is time to not only quit grumbling, quarreling, and complaining but to give thanks in all things. Why be upset when things do not go your way? There will come a better day. Why not obey Philippians 2:14 instead of skipping over it, finding an easier scripture to obey. Paul said, "Do all things without murmurings and disputings."

The opposite of murmuring is to be thankful. Do you have the right to grumble about some things and to be thankful for others? My question will be answered with scripture: "In every thing give thanks: for this is the will of God in Christ Jesus concerning you" (I Thessalonians 5:18). There is the answer! It is not man's way or understanding, but it is God's and He knows what makes the body and spirit feel good. It sure is not a complaining attitude! So why not obey Him? Because it is not natural. It has to be worked at in a conscious manner. You cannot just leave it alone, hoping it will come to pass.

It is like a can of nails that sits on the porch. The owner of the house says to the nails in the can, "You have been sitting in that can for three weeks now. Why haven't you nailed yourself into those two-by-fours and started working on that barn that needs to be built?"

If anyone heard you talking to nails that way, they would think you had slipped a cog. Just as ridiculous as it is for a nail to nail itself, so it is for a thought pattern or habit to be established by itself. Just as you are the one that must nail the nail, you are the one that must start changing a negative pattern and start building a new positive, strengthening one.

It is essential to give thanks in everything and for all things according to Ephesians 5:20: "Giving thanks always for all things unto God and the Father in the name of our Lord Jesus Christ." You can always say, "Thank You, God, for helping me get out of this difficult situation that I am placed in. Thank You for Your grace and courage that You are giving me right now to learn of You during this time of weariness and trial."

Someone once suggested to do three things when you are tempted to complain. First, look up at the heavens and remember that the main business is to get there. Secondly, look down at the earth and remind yourself how small a place you shall occupy when you die and are buried. Thirdly, look around you and observe the multitudes of people that are worse off than you. Then you will realize that complaining is wasted effort and changes nothing but your own state of mind.

The Lord God showed His great displeasure with the children of Israel when they complained. He was so angry that He caused fire to consume them.

> And when the people complained, it displeased the Lord: and the Lord heard it; and his anger was kindled: and the fire of the Lord burnt among them, and consumed them that were in the uttermost parts of the camp. And the people cried unto Moses; and when Moses prayed unto the Lord, the fire was quenched (Numbers 11:1-3).

God had taken care of them, but they were dissatisfied with His provisions. They did not like going through the wilderness and eating what God provided for them. They were thoroughly dissatisfied and let everybody know about it. Their complaining attitude added to their great weariness and distress. It totally would have wiped them out if the hand of the Lord had not been stayed.

The quickest way to deplete energy and become fixed in a cycle of weariness is to constantly fret and complain. If I could, I would shout at the top of my lungs to all complainers near and far, "Stop Complaining!" It will be the death of you if you keep it up.

If you are not sure of what you talk about and the tone of voice you use around your house, put a tape in the tape recorder and record yourself for a few days. If there is not complaining on the tape, then you are O.K. on this particular thief of energy.

AN ANGRY ATTITUDE

Every time you give vent to anger you throw some of the most important of your physical organs out of gear. This lessens your efficiency and endangers your health. It has been scientifically proven that anger completely paralyzes for the time being the workings of your stomach and other digestive organs. The glands that secrete saliva and gastric juice go instantly on strike. The muscles of the stomach become inert. Inactivity reigns through the intestinal tract.

Consequently the person who eats while he is angry, or soon after he has been angry, oftentimes suffers from an attack of indigestion. Anger also causes the liver to work overtime, pumping sugar into the blood. Thus the blood remains to some extent burdened with the excess of sugar his angry feeling has caused the liver to discharge. If he feels angry very often there may be a failure to effect gradual elimination of the surplus sugar through the kidneys. Also, the emotion of anger causes the blood to rush from the stomach to the limbs and to the brain. It increases the heartbeat and strains the blood vessels.

Instead of wasting your energy on anger, determine to rise above its insane demands. Refuse to submit to the slavery of a bad temper, for it will poison your body and pollute your heart. Someone once said, "He is happy whose circumstances suit his temper; but he is more excellent who can suit his temper to any circumstances."

George Sheehan shares a factual story that proves this. He was standing next to a runner, who was also his friend, at the awards ceremony.

"I lost my temper," said the runner next to me, "and then I lost the race."

We were standing at the awards ceremony. The winner had been announced. He was short, and thin, and he moved quietly through the crowd to collect his prize. He looked smaller and weaker than the tall, muscular young man beside me.

The second-place finisher stepped forward, then two others, then my friend's name was announced. Although he had come to win, he had never been a factor in this race.

Later he told me what had happened: "I started out in front and at a good pace. Then this guy who won jumped in front of me and slowed down. I passed him right back, but he did the same thing over and over again. Finally, I got so mad that I actually gave him a shove."

From then on, the loser had more and more difficulty maintaining the pace. Other runners glided past him. After a season of fine performances, he turned in his worst effort.

It's an old lesson: Never get angry at another runner. Rage and anger are self-defeating. These emotions create overwhelming tension that makes the task seem more difficult than it should be. [2]

ATTITUDE OF FAITH

An attitude of faith is essential. Without faith it is impossible to please God and doubt has a greater chance to rest in your brain along with the question, "Is it really worth it?"

Napoleon, one of the greatest military leaders, who also had boundless energy, uttered these profound words:

> I know men, and I tell you that Jesus is not a man. The religion of Christ is a mystery which subsists by its own force, and proceeds from a mind which is not a human mind. We find in it a marked individuality, which originated a train of words, and actions unknown before. Jesus is not a philosopher, for His proofs are miracles, and from the first His disciples adored Him.
>
> Alexander, Caesar, Charlemagne and myself founded empires: but on what foundation did we rest the creatures of our genius? Upon force. But Jesus Christ founded an empire upon love; and at this hour millions of men would die for Him.
>
> I die before my time, and my body will be given back to the earth to become food for worms. Such is the fate of him who has misery and the eternal kingdom of Christ, which is proclaimed, loved, adored and is still existing over the whole earth! [Then turning to General Berrand, the emperor added] If you do not perceive that Jesus Christ is God I did wrong in appointing you a general. [3]

Jesus based His whole kingdom on faith. He continually was either commanding them to have faith or He was showing His disappointment over their lack of faith. He repeated over and over the need for faith.

Joy Haney / What Do You Do...?

"And all things, whatsoever ye shall ask in prayer, believing, ye shall receive" (Matthew 21:22).

"Therefore I say unto you, What things soever ye desire, when ye pray, believe that ye receive them, and ye shall have them" (Mark 11:24).

When the two blind men asked Jesus to heal them, He asked, "Believe ye that I am able to do this? They said unto him, Yea, Lord. Then touched he their eyes, saying, According to your faith be it unto you" (Matthew 9:28-29).

The angel said it to Mary. "For with God nothing shall be impossible" (Luke 1:37). If you have need to be rejuvenated, look to God! He will wash that weary spirit away, if you believe. Faith is like liquid fire in your veins. It burns all the debris of tiredness that obstructs its way.

RIGHT MOTIVES

Jesus speaks in Matthew 6 that our reason for giving, praying, fasting, and doing should not be done to please men or impress them, but that it should be done to please the Lord. Sometimes our weariness is because we forget why we are doing things and get disgusted because people do not appreciate us or expect too much out of us. It is not the people, it is God whom we should be trying to please. Your main motive is that He has put it into your heart to do, so do it!

MY WORLD TASK

Let me but do my work from day to day
In field or forest, at the desk or loom,
In roaring market place or tranquil room;
Let me but find it in my heart to say,
When vagrant wishes beckon me astray,

"This is my work; my blessing, not my doom,
Of all who live, I am the one by whom
This work can best be done in the right way."
Then shall I see it not too great, not small
To suit my spirit and to prove my powers;
Then shall I, cheerful, greet the laboring hours,
And cheerful turn, when the long shadows fall,
At eventide, to play and love and rest
Because I know for me my work is best.

Van Dyke [4]

STAND-UP-AND-FIGHT ATTITUDE

"Many of our troubles are God dragging us, and they would end if we would stand upon our feet and go whither He would have us" (Henry Ward Beecher).

Are you going to give in when others say it cannot be done, or are you going to roll up your sleeves and do it, as well portrayed in the poem by Edgar A. Guest:

Somebody said that it couldn't be done,
But he with a chuckle replied
That "maybe it couldn't," but he would be one
Who wouldn't say so till he'd tried,
So he buckled right in with the trace of a grin
On his face. If he worried he hid it.
He started to sing as he tackled the thing
That couldn't be done, and he did it.

Somebody scoffed, "Oh, you'll never do that;
At least no one ever has done it";
But he took off his coat and he took off his hat,

And the first thing we knew he'd begun it.
With a lift of his chin and a bit of a grin,
Without any doubting or quiddit,
He started to sing as he tackled the thing
That couldn't be done, and he did it.

There are thousands to tell you it cannot be done,
There are thousands to prophesy failure;
There are thousands to point out to you, one by one,
The dangers that wait to assail you.
But just buckle in with a bit of a grin,
Just take off your coat and go to it;
Just start to sing as you tackle the thing
That "cannot be done," and you'll do it. [5]

Paul gives the secret how to fight and win. "Be strong in the Lord, and in the power of his might" (Ephesians 6:10). Not strong in yourself, but strong in God! This is not time to give in, but it is the era to be strong. These are difficult days, but they are days of destiny, calling forth our best effort. Be strong! We are not here to play or drift, for there is hard work to do and loads to lift. Do not just think because the days are evil that it is time to fold the hands. It matters not how things are or how hard the battle goes, just fight on.

My husband tells the story about two men who were out in the mountains walking toward a distant village, when suddenly a snowstorm came violently upon them. The blizzard was so bad that they could hardly walk. They kept stumbling and fighting their way through the storm toward the village that they knew to be somewhere in the distance. As they walked, they stumbled over a large object. Reaching down to check and see what it was, they discovered another man's body. They felt to see if there was still a heartbeat, and to their surprise they could feel a faint pulse.

One of the men looked at the other and said, "Help me pick him up. We will carry him with us to the village."

The other man said, "I cannot carry him. I am having a hard enough time making it myself."

The first man said, "Well, if you won't help me carry him, at least help me pick him up and put him on my shoulder."

So together they heaved the body upon the shoulder of the kind-hearted man, and started walking toward their destination. As the snow flurries increased, somehow the two men became separated and it seemed like they both were lost. But as the man with the load on his shoulder kept walking, weary and worn, almost ready to faint from the dead-weight on his shoulder, he saw a welcome sight in the distance: a light.

As he wearily stumbled into the village, the villagers came toward him and helped him remove his burden. He then fell upon the ground. The attending physician shook his head in amazement that the man was alive. He told the little audience that had gathered about him, "The reason this man is alive is because of the burden he carried on his back. If he had not exerted effort which caused warmth to be carried through his body, he would have died on the trail. The body heat created between the two bodies helped both of them sustain life."

The sad ending of the story is that, after the storm, they discovered the frozen body of the other man who had refused to help an unconscious man, because of his own desire to save only himself.

If you are going to win in these difficult days, it is because you carry someone along with you. You cannot be consistently worrying about yourself, ignoring those in need about you. You must live with the life-saving glow. It is time to rise up, help one another, join together, fight the forces of hell and win!

"In the world ye shall have tribulation: but be of good cheer; I have overcome the world."

Jesus, the Lord

16

Serve the Lord With Gladness

**"This is the day which the Lord hath made; we will rejoice
and be glad" (Psalm 118:24)**

Every day hath toil and trouble,
Every heart hath care;
Meekly bear thine own full measure
And thy brother's share.

Fear not, shrink not, though the burden
Heavy to thee prove:
God shall fill thy heart with GLADNESS,
And thy mouth with love.

Labor! wait! though midnight shadows
Gather round thee here,
And the storm above thee, lowering,
Fill thy heart with fear.

Wait in hope! The morning dawneth
When the night is gone,
And a peaceful rest awaits thee
When thy work is done.
                    Anonymous

A CHEERFUL ATTITUDE

An attitude of cheerfulness can often prevent weariness. An ounce of prevention is worth a pound of cure. It is better to try not to become weary, than to wait until one does. This is preventive medicine. "A merry heart doeth good like a medicine" (Proverbs 17:22). Not only is it good prevention, but it is also a good medicine for weariness. Either way you look at it, it is a winner!

Work that is cheerfully done is usually well done. A person that is grateful for the opportunity to act, to work, to love, and to serve, is one of the happiest people on earth. It is not a drudge, with the feeling of, "I have to do this," but it is an opportunity.

There are people who live under circumstances that would madden many, but because of a cheerful frame of mind and a positive philosophy of life they make it through the rough times singing instead of cursing or throwing their hands up in despair. Life calls for conquerors. Conquerors are those who triumphantly overcome a difficult situation with grace. Anyone can laugh when there is something to laugh about, or when the pockets are full of money. It is an easy thing to be cheerful when all is going well, but what about when you do not feel like it? Emil Carl Aurin shares the following poem entitled, *The Conqueror,* which mirrors this thought well:

It's easy to laugh when the skies are blue
And the sun is shining bright;
Yes, easy to laugh when your friends are true
And there's happiness in sight;
But when hope has fled and the skies are gray,
And the friends of the past have turned away,
Ah, then indeed it's a hero's feat

To conjure a smile in the face of defeat.

It's easy to laugh when the storm is o'er
And your ship is safe in port;
Yes, easy to laugh when you're on the shore
Secure from the tempest's sport;
But when wild waves wash o'er the storm-swept deck
And your gallant ship is a battered wreck,
Ah, that is the time when it's well worth while
To look in the face of defeat with a smile!

It's easy to laugh when the battle's fought
And you know that the victory's won;
Yes, easy to laugh when the prize you sought
Is yours when the race is run;
But here's to the man who can laugh when the blast
Of adversity blows; he will conquer at last,
For the hardest man in the world to beat
Is the man who can laugh in the face of defeat. [1]

Cheerfulness and contentment walk hand-in-hand. When discontent is introduced into the picture, cheerfulness exits and suspicion enters. The scene changes from a cheerful contented atmosphere to a disgruntled mess. Whatever you are asked to do, do it with all your might cheerfully. Do not always be looking around thinking maybe you should be doing so-and-so's job, and that maybe he should be doing yours. If you do whatever you are doing faithfully, and God wants to change places with you and someone else, it will come to pass. Just wait cheerfully. If God does it, it will be right; if man gets ahead of God, then disaster strikes.

There is an old Persian fable of a hen, a mouse, and a rabbit who lived happily together sharing all the work. The rabbit cooked the meals, the hen carried in the firewood, and the mouse brought the water from the nearby brook. Each did his work faithfully and contentedly.

One day while the hen was going to the forest for wood, a busybody crow asked her what she was doing. After the hen told her, the crow complained that the hen was doing the hardest part of the work and that the rabbit and mouse were doing the easy part.

Try as she might to ignore it, the thought kept rankling in the hen's mind, and when she returned home with her load of wood and her still heavier load of discontent, she cackled, "I do the hardest work ever. We ought to change our jobs."

Discontent spreads, and immediately the rabbit and mouse also thought they had been doing the hardest work. They all decided to change jobs: the mouse would cook, the rabbit would gather firewood, and the hen would bring the water.

As the rabbit hopped into the woods, a big fox trailed him, caught him, and ate him. The hen put the pail into the creek, but the current pulled the pail down under and the hen with it. The mouse wondered why they had not came back, and while he sat on the edge of the pan wondering and worrying, he lost his balance and fell into the pot of soup. Through discontent all three lost not only their happiness and sense of well-being, but also their very lives. [2]

If you desire to become weary, just lose your cheerful contentment and your wish will be granted. Shirili Muslimov allegedly lived to be 161 in Azerbaidzhan, Russia. He told an interviewer just before his death,

I am often asked for my secret of longevity, but in my opinion there is no such secret. I have toiled all my life, as a shepherd and an orchard tiller. My food consists of vegetables, fruit, milk, and bread made of coarse-milled flour. I have never over-eaten, have never smoked, nor have I ever tasted alcohol. They say that I am of *pleasant nature and merry disposition*. Also, I trust people." [3]

ATTITUDE OF DELIGHT

If at all possible, sing, hum, or whistle while you work. Work is made a joy when one goes about it with singing. Songs are contagious; sing a song and another will catch it, up and down the street it will go. Years ago a delivery boy ran up the steps of a home whistling, *Brighten the Corner Where You Are* and the lady there took it up. She was sweeping off her porch and was whistling that melody. The lady next door took it up and was singing it when finally down the street it went as if on wings of gladness—all because a young boy gave vent to the joy in his heart.

If a wren can cling to a spray a-swing,
In a mad May wind, and sing, and sing,
As if she'd burst for joy;
Why cannot I, contented lie,
In His quiet arms, beneath His sky,
Unmoved by earth's annoy? [4]

Enjoy the music of the brass instruments, the organs, pianos, violins and more. Do not forget to include music low and sweet, deep and grand, with rich harmonies that soothe away weariness. Turn the music on in your heart and sing.

Do not only sing and listen to music, but look for the beauty in things. Beauty is found in color, form and fragrance. The flowers, orchards, forests, rivers, oceans and mountains are some of the many things which make the heart of man sense a symphony within. The night with its silvery moon, beckoning stars, the whispering winds, the roar and grandeur of the storms and the seasons are all a part of the world of nature that brings a delight to the spirit of man. How sad when mankind is blind and dead to the gifts that God has placed all around him, seeing only the dreary and the mundane instead of the wonder.

Nature is full of music. The whir of wings, the whispering, wailing winds, the swish of waves, the sighing pines, the songs of birds all fill the earth with glorious symphony. If you lose the capacity to love good music and fail to hear it in nature around you, you have lost something precious that will make you very weary, for music feeds the soul.

At one time Leopold Stokowski conducted a series of concerts in Paris. As time went on he became aware of a deeper and deeper expression of gloom on the concert-master's face. Finally, curious as to the cause of such profound melancholy, Stokowski began to question the man.

"Tell me, my friend," he said, "why are you so unhappy? Are you having domestic troubles, or do you feel unwell? Or perhaps you're in some financial difficulty?"

"No, no," growled the concert-master, "I detest music!"

What a predicament! His life's career smack dab in the middle of something he hated. The problem was not the music; the problem was his attitude. It is not enough to be successful in what you are doing, but to live simply and cheerfully while you are doing it.

This is Success.
To live well. To laugh often. To love much.
To gain the respect of others.
To win the love of little children.
To fill one's niche and accomplish one's task.
To leave the world better than one finds it,
whether by an improved flower, a perfect poem

or another life ennobled.
To never lack appreciation of earth's beauty
or fail to express it.
To always look for the best in others.
To give the best one has.
To make one's life an inspiration
and one's memory a benediction. [5]

You may say, "I don't feel like singing." Sing anyway! Scientific evidence proves that the body is affected by what the mind dwells upon, by singing and by the spoken word. That is why in many hospitals today patients are encouraged to listen to positive tapes while they are in the hospital; it affects the healing process.

It is an established fact that you will have days when you feel like quitting, nothing will go right and the sun will be hidden, making things appear grayer than they really are. Just as there are seasons in the earth, there are seasons in your life. There are dips and highs, lows and sighs; yes, it will not always be a season that is conducive to being jolly. This is not the time to give up, but to smile gently and go on towards the goal.

Bitter and bleak is the closing day;
The wind goes wailing, the sky is gray,
And there's never a bird or bough or spray—
Alas, how dreary!
But summer will surely come again.
The earth needs snow and cold and rain,
Just as our hearts need grief and pain.
And so be cheery.

James Buckham [6]

"Our body is a well-set clock, which keeps good time, but if it be too much or indiscreetly tampered with, the alarm runs out before the hour."

Joseph Hall

17

Eat and Run

"I wish above all things that thou mayest prosper and in health" (III John 2)

"Wars are won by men with strong wills and strong bodies!" said the colorful World War II general, George Patton, who always stressed physical fitness. He said, "A strong will to win is more important than a strong body! Men have won battles when totally exhausted and near death from injuries. However, that will to win did not get into the brain without first having a strong body. You have to keep the body active to keep all of the juices running to the right places." [1]

He demanded that every man run a mile every day when not in active duty. He would tell men who were sitting doing desk work, "Get up and get out of here! Check on the troops and the trucks! Keep moving around so the juices of the body will run to the right places, especially the brain. If you sit there too long all of the brain power will be in your shoes. You cannot keep your mind active when your body is inactive." [2]

He would give them pep talks that were certainly unorthodox, but he inspired his men with such talks as this one: "In war, as in everything else, a man needs all of the brains he can get. Nobody ever had too many brains. Brains come from oxygen. Oxygen comes from the lungs where the air goes. This oxygen in the air gets into the blood and travels to the brain. So breathe deeply." [3]

Porter B. Williamson, the author who shared special insights about General Patton, writes,

I remembered General Patton's advice when in 1968 one of the top doctors in the space program talked of the problems of exercise for astronauts. This doctor stated that research had indicated that the muscles will not gain in strength by doing something which can be done easily. "To gain strength," the doctor reported, "the body must be exerted to the point of exhaustion and go on." I stopped listening to the space doctor because my mind was racing back to the tall figure of General Patton giving the same advice over twenty-five years earlier. [4]

If you are suffering from weariness, try running and exercising your way out of it. I remember several years ago reading the story of housewife who had three or four children and two of them were twins. By the end of the day she was ready to tear her hair out. She was tired, restless, and weary, but she read an article on the powerful effects running had on the body and brain. So she told her husband, "When you get home from work I am running out the door while you stay with the kids."

This she did. When he got home she was waiting with her tennis shoes on. She said she felt a euphoric glow move through her body after running. As she ran, the tensions and weariness seem to run out through her feet and onto the ground. As a result of this daily exercise, she became an efficient new woman with a new outlook on life. Her weariness

Joy Haney / What Do You Do...?

disappeared and she once again enjoyed being with her children; life took on new meaning.

"Body, Mind and Soul are inextricably woven together," says cardiologist Paul Dudley White, "and whatever helps or hurts one of these three...helps or hurts the other two." [5]

Physician Linda Weinreb, who maintains a private practice, makes rounds at a local hospital and works in a free clinic, discussed the effects of conditioning on her attitude: "When I don't exercise I'm lethargic and disengaged. I get irritable much more easily and tire more quickly. When I exercise regularly I'm more vital and positive. I have a feeling of fullness. I'm more present for my patients and my work is much better." [6]

"A healthy body is a guest chamber for the soul; a sick body is a prison," says Francis Bacon. Your health is important. O.S. Marden wrote the following essay over 75 years ago that still is applicable today:

I AM...?

A life and happiness builder.

I bring out the best that is in you.

I restore lost courage and stamina, and help you to live up to your ideals.

I am that which keeps you fit, always at the top of your condition. And to keep fit, physically and mentally, is the secret of success and happiness.

I am one of the prime necessities of a normal life, that which helps to lay the foundations of your career, your health and well-being.

I iron out your wrinkles, rid you of care and worry lines, take years off your life.

I clarify your ideas, strengthen your purpose, renew your ideals and raise your standards all along the line of your physical and mental being.

I have helped millions to find that "other self," the bigger man or woman that was buried under the accumulated cares and anxieties of business and family life.

I do more to add to your attractiveness than all the beauty aids in the world.

I make you a healthier, saner, sounder, more vigorous, more efficient man or woman, one who works on the lever of his strength instead of his weakness, who uses the bigger self instead of the little inefficient fellow who spoils so many lives.

You can't afford to neglect me, for I play a most important part in the work of brain and body building. Without me life becomes a dull mechanical grind. You become a machine. You don't live; you only exist. I enlarge your horizon, give you a new outlook.

I am an insurance against pessimism, the "blues" and physical bankruptcy. I enable you to store up reserve power which carries you safely through tremendous emergencies, great crises in the battle of life. Without the reserve that I give, you would go down to defeat.

I am the great antidote for depleted vitality, the thing which breeds nervousness, doubt, hesitation, timidity, uncertainty, vacillation—all the foes of success. I build assurance, self-confidence, boldness, decision, promptness, courage—all the positive success qualities.

I make you fit for the battle of life. Every now and then nations talk a great deal about "preparedness." I am one of the surest means for building up your life defenses, making you ready for enterprises that demand the qualities of the good soldier—courage, endurance, patience, energy, resourcefulness, persistence, the will to win.

I am that which enables you to get the most out of life because I help you to put the most into it. I multiply your achievement and your happiness by multiplying your ability, jacking up your manhood, your womanhood, your physical and spiritual being, by right living, right eating, right thinking, right recreation, right exercise.

I AM HEALTH! [7]

What an essay! You might ask, "How could health do all that?" and "Is it biblical?" First of all ask yourself what can you do if you are hooked up to a machine with ill health or experiencing constant pain in your body. Does sickness distract from accomplishing things? Is it difficult to live in a positive mood where there is prolonged sickness? Does the opposite of health affect the emotions negatively?

I am sure you will agree that an unhealthy body distracts from life rather than adds to it. Does the Bible have any direction as to the condition of health in the body? Is it important enough for God to discuss it?

It is important to God for it is discussed often in the scriptures. The New Testament gives certain direction as to the will of God for all mankind. III John 2 says, "Beloved, I wish above all things that thou mayest prosper and be in health, even as thy soul prospereth."

It is a fact that health is to be considered a number one priority because the condition of your mind and body affects all that you do. *Above all things!* That puts your health on the top line, but He did not just emphasize the health of the body. First of all, there was the soul prosperity which is always number one. Then He desired for the body to be in health as the soul prospered. One affects the other.

What you say affects the health of the body. "...The tongue of the wise is health" (Proverbs 12:18). Other scriptures allude to the fact that the tongue influences other bodily parts. It is essential to speak wisely and with biblical understanding, for in doing so, one is speaking health into the body. Speaking and thinking do affect the health of a person.

God often makes it possible to live in health, but man pollutes his body with negative talk, thinking that is not based on the Bible, and food that has been depleted of vitamins and minerals. He lives any old way, develops habits which do not promote health, and then expects to be in top condition. It just does not work that way. Sooner or later all things require just dues. What you put in will eventually seed and produce, whether good or evil.

FOOD DOES MAKE A DIFFERENCE

Carbohydrates are the main suppliers of the body's energy. During digestion, starches and sugars, the principal kinds of carbohydrates, are broken down into glucose, better known as blood sugar. This blood sugar provides the essential energy for the brain and central nervous system. If you eat too many carbohydrates, more than can be converted into glucose or glycogen, which is stored in the liver and muscles, the result is fat.

There are many vitamin-rich and mineral-rich starch and sugar foods which will give your body quick energy . You will find them in whole grains, whole breads, whole wheat pastas, root vegetables, sweet fruits, vegetables and their juices. Nature's own sweeteners include golden honey, real maple syrup, and sun-dried fruits such as apricots, figs and dates.

Overrefined sugar products come to you emptied of vitamins and minerals. To metabolize them, to burn them into energy—which is all they are good for—your body must use its precious B vitamins, and B vitamins give you energy also. Make every bite count; this is where discipline enters the picture again.

A good diet of lean meats, fish, vegetables, fruits, seeds and grains, coupled with a daily intake of Vitamins A, B, C, and E and a multi-mineral capsule will strengthen the body and give it proper energy for performing daily duties. Conversely a daily diet of sodas, candy bars, chips, pies, cakes and fried and heavily oiled meats and vegetables will deplete the energy.

Improper food intake is not the only thing that will deplete energy. Stress is a number one factor. That is why many nutritional books encourage a teaspoon of ascorbic acid to be taken daily as a prevention against colds and flu, which result often after a severe time of anxiety or stress. Stress kills Vitamin C in the body and tears down resistance against disease. Since the body does not manufacture Vitamin C, it must be taken orally every day.

> Tranquilizers, pep pills and barbiturates merely mask, not correct, emotional tensions. Safe nutritional substances include calcium, lecithin, the entire Vitamin B complexes and Vitamin C. After a shock of any kind, the Vitamin C reserve stored in your adrenal glands is exhausted within minutes. By replacing Vitamin C in massive doses, the normal level in the body is restored. Vitamin C protects against infection and other disturbances. [8]

If you are always tired, and are depending on such crutches to keep you going such as pep pills, coffee by the bucket, aspirin or tranquilizers, you can change all that. You can gain vibrant energy and look as vital as you feel. Examine what you are eating, if you are getting enough exercise, sleep habits and such.   It is possible that your weariness stems from these factors.

EPILOGUE

Maybe you have the mistaken notion that the race Paul talked about would be easy. Maybe you have approached it with a laid-back attitude. Are you putting things off until tomorrow when you did not feel like it today? Paul said, "And every man that striveth for the mastery is temperate in all things. Now they do it to obtain a corruptible crown; but we an incorruptible. I therefore so run, not as uncertainly: so fight I, not as one that beateth the air: But I keep under my body, and bring it into subjection" (I Corinthians 9:25-27).

This portrays someone trying to master something to attain a crown, but in so doing, he shows discipline, subjection and purpose. When you became God's child, you entered into a fight for your life. Instead of going downhill into all that self-destructs, you are asked to start walking upward toward God. Your enemies, the devil and your flesh, do not like you to put off the old man that would bring you down, but Paul said if you are going to win you will war in the spirit. When you look at Old Testament figures who warred against evil you see the end result. While they were warring they did not see the end result, but kept their integrity with God. They simply did not become weary in well doing, but stayed in there as long as it took, and it was well worth the effort. Look at the pattern of four Old Testament leaders:

David was anointed to be King (I Samuel 16:13), then someone tried to kill him (I Samuel 20:33). It was not an easy road for him.

Esther was chosen to be Queen (Esther 2:17); now she was going to die (Esther 3:13).

Daniel was elected second-in-command (Daniel 2:48); now he was going to be eaten by lions (Daniel 6:3).

Joseph had a dream of leading (Genesis 37:5); now he was going to die (Genesis 37:28).

The day of their anointing, coronation, promotion, or dreaming was great and wonderful, but the testing time was just around the corner. So it is still today; everything has its cycles. First, the exuberance, then the valley, the testing, the trial, the opposition and the frustrated purpose. This is where decisions that affect destinies are made. To either give into weariness and quit, or keep plodding on no matter what, is the choice that must be made.

David, Esther, Daniel and Joseph had much in common. They all had dreams of grandeur, power, and authority, but their leadership was tested before they arrived there. You will have disappointments that will invoke weariness, but just get up and go again. It is not the sitting down that matters, but it is how long you sit. It is not the falling down that determines what happens to you, it is how long you stay there or if you even get up. It also depends on what kind of attitude you have when you do get up.

You will encounter weariness before you accomplish that which God has asked you to do, but it is just temporary. The fragrance of your life is made up of many experiences, so mix it well and let it send forth an aroma pleasing unto God. You are going to make it, if you will just keep going...*in spite of!*

Notes

Chapter 1

1. Arranged and Compiled by Dean C. Dutton, Ph.D., *Quests and Conquests* (Guthrie, OK: Live Service Publishing Co., 1923), #390.

Chapter 2

1. Dutton, #461
2. Helen Keller, *The Story of my Life*, (New York, NY: Airmont Publishing Co. 1965) p. 39
3. Paul Lee Tan, ThD., *Encyclopedia of 7,700 Illustrations: Signs of the Times* (Rockville, Maryland: Assurance Publishers, 1979), p. 1674
4. Dutton, #165

Chapter 3

1. Dutton, #139
2. Ibid., #1165
3. Ibid., #1158
4. Robert G. Lee, D.D., *Quotable Illustrations*, (Grand Rapids, MI: Zondervan Publishing House, 1962), p. 48-49

Chapter 4

1. Dutton, #965.
2. Ibid., #230
3. Ibid.. #228
4. Ibid.. #925

5.   Elizabeth Rice Hanford, *Your Clothes Say It for You*, (Murfreesboro, TN: Sword of the Lord Publishers, 1976), p. 25
6.   Tan, p. 775.
7.   Terrence Des Pres, *The Survivor, An Anatomy of Life in the Death Camps*, (New York, N.Y.: Oxford University Press, c. 1976). p, 63
8.   Des Pres, p. 63

Chapter 5

1.   Dutton, #495-A.
2.   Ibid., #173
3.   Tan, p.1358.
4.   Tan, p. 1508
5.   Tan, p. 1508
6.   Lee, p. 92

Chapter 6

1.   Dutton, #1230
2.   Ibid., #1233
3.   Joseph S. Johnson, *A Field of Diamonds*, (Broadman Press, Nashville, TN: c. 1974) p. 152
4.   Dutton, #495
5.   Ibid., #891
6.   Ibid., #1158
7.   Ibid., #492
8.   Ibid., #302
9.   Ibid., #470
10. Lee, p. 102
11. Ibid., p. 103

Chapter 7

1. Dutton, #227.
2. Tan, p. 186
3. Ibid. p. 188

Chapter 8

1. Tan, p. 1642
2. Dutton, #188-B.
3. Edited by Clinton T. Howell, *Lines to Live By* (Nashville, TN: Thomas Nelson Publishers, 1972), p. 184

Chapter 9

1. Dutton, #94-B.
2. Ibid., #407.
3. Ibid., #498
4. Lillian Eichler Watson, ed. & comm., *Light from Many Lamps* (New York, NY: Simon & Schuster, 1951), p. 6
5. Dutton, #220-A.

Chapter 10

1. Howell, p. 49
2. Dutton, #186
3. Ibid. #168

Chapter 11

1. Dutton, #42
2. Tan, p. 984
3. Watson, p. 220

4. Hazel Felleman, selected by, *The Best Loved Poems of the American People* (Garden City, NY: Doubleday & Co., Inc. 1936) p.137.

Chapter 12

1. Dutton, #1071-C.
2. Ibid., #596
3. Ibid., #98
4. Felleman, p. 113.
5. Howell, p. 156.
6. Felleman, p. 88.

Chapter 13

1. Frank Bettger, *How I Raised Myself from Failure to Success in Selling*, (Englewood Cliffs, NJ: Prentice-Hall, Inc., 1949) p. 5
2. Ibid. p. 9
3. Ibid. p. 10
4. Dutton, #70.

Chapter 14

1. Felleman, p. 122.

Chapter 15

1. Dutton, #92.
2. Sheehan, George, M.D., *George Sheehan on Running to Win*, (Emmaus, PA: Rodale Press, 1992). p. 197
3. Dutton, #1135
4. Ibid., #358

5. Edgar A. Guest, *Collected Verse of Edgar A. Guest* (Chicago, IL: The Reilly & Lee Co., 1934) p. 285.

Chapter 16

1. Dutton, #926
2. Tan, p. 256.
3. Ibid., p. 933.
4. Dutton, #5.
5. Ibid., #502
6. Ibid., #94-B

Chapter 17

1. Porter B. Williamson, *Patton's Principles, A Handbook for Managers Who Mean It*, (New York, NY: Simon and Schuster, 1979), p.53.
2. Ibid., p. 54
3. Ibid., p. 55
4. Ibid., p. 64
5. Robert J. Kriegel, Ph.D., Marilyn Kriegel, Ph.D., *The C Zone Peak Performance Under Pressure*, (Garden City, NY: Anchor Press, Doubleday, 1984). p. 114
6. Ibid., p. 115
7. Dutton, #188A
8. Clark, Linda A., M.A., *Secrets of Health and Beauty*, (New York, NY: Jove Publications, 1969).